FIXED-INCOME PORTFOLIO MANAGEMENT
ISSUES AND SOLUTIONS

FIXED-INCOME PORTFOLIO MANAGEMENT
ISSUES AND SOLUTIONS

edited by
Thomas S. Y. Ho

Proceedings from the
First Annual GAT Conference

BUSINESS ONE IRWIN
Homewood, Illinois 60430

Project editor: Karen Nelson
Production manager: Ann Cassady
Compositor: EmDash Words & Graphics, New York, N.Y.
Typeface: 10/12 Times Roman
Printer: Book Press, Inc.

Library of Congress Cataloging-in-Publication Data

Fixed-income portfolio management: issues and solutions / edited by
Thomas S. Y. Ho.
  p.   cm.
 ISBN 1-55623-845-2
 1. Fixed-income securities—Congresses. 2. Portfolio management-
-Congresses.
 HG4651.F577 1993
 332.63'2044—dc20   92–37516

Printed in the United States of America

    1 2 3 4 5 6 7 8 9 0   B P 9 8 7 6 5 4 3 2

PREFACE

In March 1992, GAT held its first annual Fixed-Income Conference at Captiva Island, Florida. The mission of the conference was a serious search for scientific approaches to fixed-income applications, focusing on the needs of buy-side managers.

The Conference brought together speakers who presented papers on topics ranging from mortgage-backed securities analytics to asset-liability management. The research ideas are thought-provoking, and they bridge the gap between state-of-the-art theory and practice. The insights of the papers reach deep into the daily work of a fixed-income manager, while maintaining a high academic standard. The presentations energized all the participants. These Proceedings compile the papers into a central theme, *Fixed-Income Management: Issues and Solutions.*

One of the most astounding changes in fixed-income markets in recent years is the growth of analytical applications. Quantitative research has dismantled the thinking that Treasuries, corporates, and insurance products are all separate markets; that matrix pricing is a necessary tool for bond valuation; and that equity portfolio theory can be easily adapted for fixed-income management. Quantitative research has brought us OAS analysis to measure relative value, pricing models based on economic theories, and many innovative bond portfolio strategies. In short, quantitative research has launched fixed-income management into a new era.

We must recognize that financial technologies and system technologies are intertwined in this new era, and they form the foundation of quantitative research. For example, consider the pricing models in historical progression. Referring to Figure 1, the Black-Scholes model, proposed in 1973, is a closed-form solution which can be computed by a calculator. By 1979, the Brennan and Schwartz bond pricing models involved computing intensive numerical methods. In 1986, Waldman's mortgage pricing model involved sampling in an astronomically large sample space. Now, we require key rate durations, large-scale optimizations, and other financial technologies in fixed-income management.

FIGURE 1

year	authors	analytics	methodology
1973	Black-Scholes	option pricing	closed form
1975	McCulloch	spot curve	linear regression
1977	Cox, Ingersoll, Ross	term structure	binomial
1979	Brennan, Schwartz	bond pricing	finite difference
1986	Ho, Lee	bond pricing	binomial
1986	Waldman	mortgage pricing	rate paths sampling
1987	Kopprasch et al	effective duration	repeated calculations
1988	Heath et al	n factor model	n factor lattice
1990	Black et al	bond pricing	binomial

The key development in system technologies has been the introduction of the microprocessor, which has led to a rapid increase in the availability of computing power and a rapid decline in the cost. In Figure 2, we present the introduction of selected microprocessors in a historical perspective, and their computing speed as measured by single-precision Whetstones. (Whetstones is the standard measure of computing speed for floating point calculations which are central in financial applications.) We can see in Figure 3 that microprocessor-based systems, first introduced around 1980, are rapidly overtaking the processing power of much more expensive mainframe systems.

FIGURE 2

year	microsystem	Whetstones single precision
1986	80286	24
1987	DSP32-16	4001
1988	80386	1860
1988	MIPS M/2000	3000
1990	VAX 4000	10633
1990	MIPS M/3000	16978
1991	80486	8808
1991	i 860	19880
1992	HP9000/730	75758

FIGURE 3
Evolution of Floating Point Computing Power and Financial Modeling

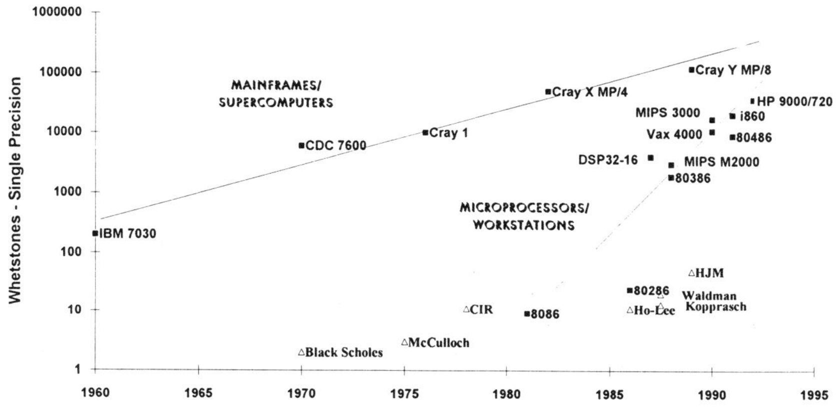

Financial technologies depend on system technologies. More readily accessible computing power enables us to further exploit quantitative research for applications. Looking ahead, the trend in technology can only continue in a more dramatic way. For those of us in fixed-income management, this era is a time of opportunity. With opportunities come issues and solutions. These proceedings address some of these topics.

In Chapter 1, Davidson analyzes the impact of the shape of the yield curve on the value of an MBS. He identifies different measures of value and explores the benefits and drawbacks of each. Chapters 2 and 3 investigate the valuation of MBS/CMOs. In Chapter 2, Ho uses the Linear Path Space approach to value CMOs, and he uses the model to analyze the embedded-option risks. In Chapter 3, Hall provides empirical tests of the Fidelilty OAS models on the returns of MBS. He shows how the results indicate increasing efficiencies in the market.

In Chapter 4, Kao extends some of the new approaches in quantitative analytics to illiquid securities. He provides a methodology to analyze credit risks in private placements and commercial mortgages. Further, he presents a procedure used at GM to specify a commercial mortgages benchmark. McCoy, in Chapter 5, extends the research to an enhanced indexation portfolio. Using key rate durations and cheap/rich analysis, McCoy empirically investigates the returns of different strategies.

The next three chapters are on asset-liability management of insurance companies. Lally presents an allocation rule to equity investment. He then extends the analysis to the specifications of liability indices and their applications. Yoon presents the step by step procedure on the asset-allocation strategies implemented at Equitable. He demonstrates the strengths and weaknesses of these approaches. McAvity applies the analysis of asset-liability management to the economic analysis of an insurance company.

I would like to thank all the speakers for their research and their cooperation in these Proceedings. These papers are serious and thoughtful works on practical applications. They are on the cutting edge of quantitative research. I believe these proceedings will bring the excitement that we experienced at the GAT Fixed-Income Conference to a broader audience.

Thomas S. Y. Ho

TABLE OF CONTENTS

CHAPTER 1

MORTGAGE-BACKED SECURITIES AND THE YIELD CURVE

Andrew S. Davidson
President, Andrew Davidson & Co., Inc.

INTRODUCTION

From May 1983 to May 1988 the spread between the ten-year treasury yield and the two-year treasury yield held within a reasonably narrow range from about 50 basis points to about 150 basis points. During the last two-years that spread has wandered widely from about minus 40 basis points to over 210 basis points. The changing shape of the yield curve has had a significant impact on the dynamics of the mortgage-backed securities (MBS) market. MBS valuation models and approaches developed during periods of less yield curve volatility may not properly measure the impact of the changing yield curve on the value of these securities.

ANALYSIS PROCESS

A standard MBS model has four basic components. First, there is an interest-rate model. Second, there is a prepayment model. Third, there is a cash-flow generator. And finally, there is a valuation process. Within this framework, academics and market participants have developed an endless variety of sophisticated tools to value MBS. The recent trend has been to develop models of greater complexity to better reflect the intricate nuances of these securities.

Andrew Davidson is President of Andrew Davidson & Co., Inc., 524 Broadway, Sixth Floor, New York, New York, 10012. The author would like to thank Tom Ho and Michael Herskovitz for their thoughtful comments. He would also like to thank Marcy Joseph and everyone at GAT for their assistance and support.

This analysis takes a different tack. Here we will look at an extremely simple mortgage model. In each phase of the analysis, we will use the simplest approach required to demonstrate how the shape of the yield curve can effect the value of MBS. First, we will develop this simplified model, and then use it to evaluate changes in MBS value under different assumptions within that simplified world.

Due to the simplicity of the model, it will be impossible to evaluate the effect of complex phenomena on MBS value. Because the model doesn't account for a wide variety of important factors that affect MBS value, this model cannot be and is not intended to be a trading tool. Rather, it provides a tool for assessing and understanding the impact of the shape of the yield curve on MBS value. The simplicity of the model allows us to gain greater insight into how changes in the shape of the yield curve can affect value, and how our choices of model assumptions can affect the results of the model.

While the model is relatively simple, the parameters have been chosen so that the results of the analysis should provide a good indication of both the direction and magnitude of the effects.

INTEREST RATES

In an MBS model, the underlying interest-rate assumptions will drive the prepayment model and the valuation process. In practice, a great degree of effort and insight goes into creating an interest-rate process that has sufficient flexibility to reflect market realities while not violating arbitrage conditions and other reasonable constraints.

In this model, our goal is to create the simplest description of the yield curve that will enable us to evaluate the impact of the shape of the yield curve on MBS value. This is really a question of determining the minimum number of parameters to include in our model. With one point, we can only vary the level of the curve. With two points, we can vary the slope of the curve. With three points, we can vary the curvature as well. To get the necessary flexibility, we will assume that the entire yield curve is driven by three rates; the one-year, the ten-year and the thirty-year. To keep the analysis simple, we will use zero coupon bonds as our benchmarks and assume linear interpolation to create the intermediate rates.

We will also assume zero volatility. That is, a world of perfect certainty. Although this assumption is extremely unrealistic, it simplifies the analysis so we can view the impact of the shape of the curve without having to also evaluate option characteristics. This analysis could be extended to include non-zero volatility, but that is beyond the scope of this paper. Remember, the goal here is to gain insight into MBS valuation, not to create a viable trading tool.

In this analysis we will concentrate on three different sets of assumptions–three different states of the world: a flat yield curve, a steep yield curve and a kinked yield curve. For each curve we can calculate a set of forward rates for bonds of each maturity. The forward rate is the rate that you can lock in today for funds to be invested for a specified maturity on that date in the future. In our simplified world, with no volatility, the forward rate is also the rate for specified maturity at a given time in the future which must occur if there are no arbitrage opportunities.

Each of the three worlds has very different forward rate patterns. Figures 1 through 3 show each of the curves and the associated path of forward rates for the one-year zero and the ten-year zero. In the flat curve scenario, all rates remain at a constant 7% over the entire period of analysis. In the steep curve, forward rates rise rapidly from their current levels, eventually exceeding even the thirty-year zero rate. The kinked curve presents the most interesting pattern. Despite the fact that the kinked curve is upwardly sloped along its entire length, the forward rates first rise, then level off, and then decline before rising again. It is the interaction of these differently shaped forward rate curves with the prepayment model that will create some of the most intriguing aspects of this analysis.

FIGURE 1
Flat Yield Curve

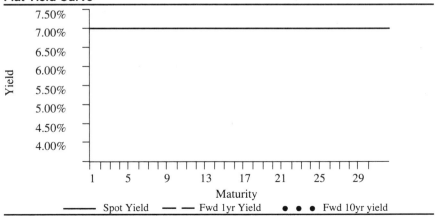

FIGURE 2
Steep Yield Curve

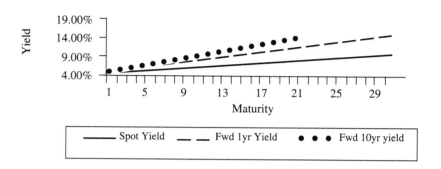

FIGURE 3
Kinked Yield Curve

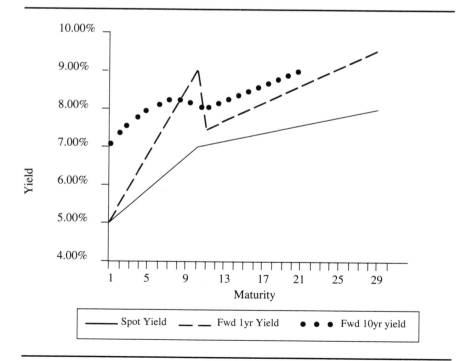

PREPAYMENTS

Prepayment modeling is extremely complex and time consuming. Recent advances in prepayment modeling have incorporated a variety of economic effects into the forecasting of prepayments. Given the complexity of prepayment modeling, the formulation for this model is embarrassingly simple.

Prepayments result from three activities; default, moving, and refinancing. We will assume that there is a base level of prepayments from moving and default, and that prepayments increase (up to a point) when borrowers can refinance into a lower coupon mortgage. To model this pattern, we will assume that the prepayment rate is a piecewise linear function of the difference between the coupon on the mortgage and the alternative financing rate. As shown in Figure 4, prepayments are constant at 5% per year if the spread is below 1%. They rise linearly to 30% as the spread increases to 3%, and then remain constant at 30% for all spreads greater than 3%. The model has no seasonality, no aging, no burnout and no housing market variables. (If only life were so simple!)

FIGURE 4
Prepayment Function

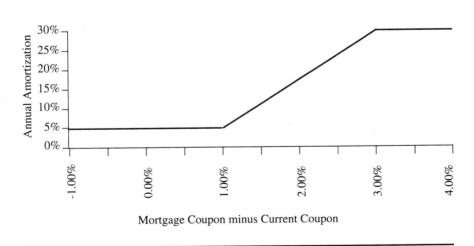

Mortgage Coupon minus Current Coupon

In the real world, refinancing is driven by the set of alternative financial vehicles available to the borrower. For most borrowers, a home mortgage is their cheapest source of borrowing. The fact that their home is their most valuable pledgable asset combined with the tax deductibility of home mortgage interest payments makes the mortgage tough competition for other forms of borrowing. Traditionally, only long term (fifteen-year and thirty-year) fixed-rate mortgages were available. However, the development of adjustable-rate mortgages (ARMs), balloon mortgages, two-step products and other innovations has expanded the range of options available to the borrower. Prior to the development of these instruments, borrowers only had viable refinancing opportunities in one sector of the yield curve (somewhere in the seven to ten-year average-life range). These new instruments have created opportunities for efficient financing all along the curve. Through these new types of mortgages the shape of the yield curve has come to have a greater impact on refinancing activity. When the yield curve steepens (the short end declines), borrowers—especially those who expect to move within a few years—opt for the lower rates afforded by these alternative instruments.

The shape of the curve also affects prepayments through the impact of discounting cash flows that occur at different times at different yields. The mechanism of the CMO facilitates this process. The CMO splits the mortgage cash flows into bonds with varying average lives and risk characteristics. This subdivision of the cash flows allows different components of the mortgage to be priced off of different parts of the yield curve. When the curve is steep, shorter tranches can be priced and sold at lower yields. The net effect is that when the yield curve steepens (assuming that short rates fall), MBS values rise and current coupon yields fall. These lower mortgage rates translate into greater refinancing opportunities.

In this model, we bypass these complex pathways and create a structure which allows us to analyze the impact of refinancing driven either by the ten-year rate alone, or by a blend of the one-year rate and the ten-year rate. The effect of the yield curve is incorporated in the model through the calculation of the alternative financing rate. The alternative refinancing rate can also be thought of as the effective mortgage current coupon which accounts for all the possible refinancing alternatives. For the single factor model the alternative financing rate is the ten-year zero rate plus a constant. For the blended-rate model the alternative financing rate is equal to 75% of the ten-year rate plus 25% of the one-year rate plus a constant. The constants are set so that in each case the starting rate equals 8%. In this way, neither the shape of the curve nor the choice of refinancing rate model affects the initial refinancing incentive. The differences in projected prepayments among the different curves stem from the shapes of the curves, not from the level of the initial refinancing opportunity.

Prepayment forecasts can be generated for each of the three yield curves. First, the forecast refinancing rate (current coupon) is calculated based on the forward rates. For the flat yield curve the refinancing rate remains constant and is the same for both the ten-year model and the blended-rate model. For the steep curve, the refinancing rate rises over time as the forward rates rise. The ten-year model and the blended-rate model produce identical refinancing rates because the slope of the one-year forward curve is the same as the slope of the ten-year forward curve. The kinked yield curve presents a much different picture. Both the ten-year model and the blended-rate models forecast generally increasing refinancing rates. However, in the blended-rate model the refinancing rate rises much more rapidly as the one-year component of the rate rises more rapidly than the ten-year component.

For any given mortgage, with a set coupon, this can be translated into a refinancing incentive. The refinancing incentive or spread can be calculated by subtracting the alternative refinancing rate from the mortgage coupon. For example, if a mortgage has a coupon of 10.5%, the spread will start at 2.5% based on a mortgage current coupon of 8%, and then decline over time as the projected zero-coupon rates rise. Figure 5 shows the forecasted spread for a 10.5% mortgage using both the ten-year and blended-rate models for the assumed kinked yield curve. Since the blended-rate model forecasts higher refinancing rates, it forecasts a lower spread.

FIGURE 5
Projected Differential

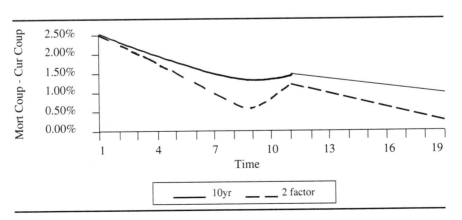

The difference in spread patterns translates into differing prepayment forecasts. Figure 6 shows the prepayment forecast vectors for the two models. As expected the blended-rate model produces much lower prepayments than the ten-year model. Here we can already begin to see how the shape of the curve coupled with our choice of modeling assumption can drive the analysis of the mortgage security. Merely by assuming that the alternative financing rate is tied to two points on the yield curve rather than just one, we can get substantially different prepayment forecasts even when we are using the same prepayment model.

FIGURE 6
Projected Prepayments

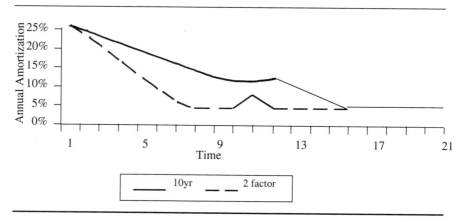

It is important to note that the source of the difference in prepayment forecasts is the shape of the forward curves. For the flat and steep curves, the ten-year and blended-rate models would produce the same prepayment forecasts. However, for the kinked curve, it only takes a slight change in the formulation of the input to the prepayment model to have a sizable impact on the prepayment forecast.

CASH FLOWS

Numerical analysis of the impact of the effect of the curve and the modeling assumptions on the value of securities requires that the prepayment model be applied to the calculation of security cash flows. For this analysis, we want a cash flow generation model that is robust enough to create a variety of securities with different performance characteristics, yet simple enough so that it does not obscure the analysis process. The cash flow generator described below follows the general pattern used in the CMO swap market and for other indexed amortizing products.

For the purpose of this analysis, we will assume that security cash flows (interest and principal) occur annually. To further simplify the analysis, prepayments are stated as a percentage of the original balance (rather than the amortized outstanding balance) and are assumed to occur only once a year. Each bond is specified by several variables:

- The underlying mortgage coupon (which will be used to calculate the refinancing incentive).
- The coupon on the bond.
- The maturity of the bond.
- The lockout period.

The cash flows of the bond are then straightforward calculations:

- The interest payment equals the coupon times the principal balance.
- The principal payment is zero during the lockout period, and is equal to the original balance times the prepayment rate until the balance is reduced to zero, and is equal to the remaining balance at maturity.

FIGURE 7
Security Cash Flows

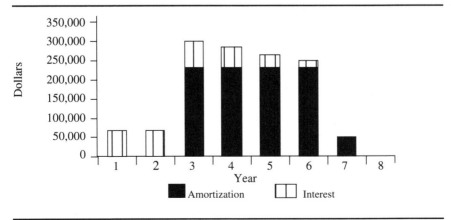

Figure 7 shows cash flows for a sample bond with a coupon of 7%, a three-year lockout (first principal payment at the end of year three), and a fifteen-year maturity, assuming a prepayment rate of 23.75% per year. Figure 8 shows the balance of that same bond, first assuming the same 23.75% prepayment rate, and then assuming a 5% prepayment rate. Under the 5% prepayment rate, the bond extends substantially.

FIGURE 8
Security Balance

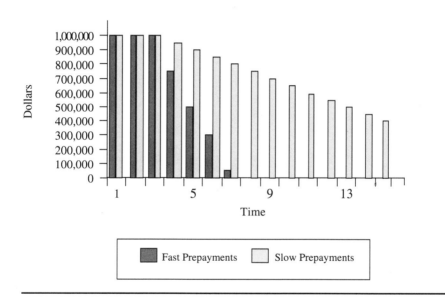

This simple cash flow generation routine provides sufficient flexibility to create bonds which have a wide range of performance characteristics. Varying the lockout and maturity will affect the stability of the bond, varying the coupon will affect the price (discount vs. premium) and varying the underlying mortgage coupon will affect the sensitivity to rate changes.

For the valuation analysis that follows, we will keep all of the characteristics as described in Figures 7 and 8, but will vary the bonds' coupons for the different yield curve environments in order to keep the price of the bond the same. In the analysis, we will concentrate on a set of par bonds (priced at 100) and a set of premium bonds (priced at 110). By constructing bonds this way, their performance will roughly match CMO payers (non-PAC, non-support bonds with intermediate maturities).

VALUATION

The valuation techniques employed here are simple. In a world without volatility there isn't much room for complex analytical tools. Three techniques will be used. All three are yield spreads of various sorts. For each method, it is necessary to choose a basis for calculating the security cash flows, and to choose an appropriate discounting method.

The first method is the *nominal* spread. The nominal yield spread is determined by calculating the yield of the bond assuming a constant prepayment rate based on the initial level of rates. For a 10.5% mortgage with an 8% current coupon, our simple prepayment model produces a 23.75% prepayment rate. The yield of the zero-coupon bond with a whole number maturity just less than the average life of the bond is subtracted from the yield of the bond. This is equivalent to the most commonly used measure of yield spread in the mortgage and CMO market, except that here we are using a zero-coupon bond rather than the on-the-run-coupon bond.

The second method is the *zero* (or spot) spread. For this calculation, the cash flows of the bond are determined as in the nominal yield method. In this method, the spread is calculated by discounting each bond cash flow by the appropriate zero rate plus a spread. The zero spread is that spread for which the discounted value of the cash flows equals the price of the bond. In practice, one usually guesses a spread and then iterates to find the correct spread.

The third method is the *forward* spread. The forward spread is determined in the same manner as the zero spread, but uses a different prepayment assumption. For the forward spread, the cash flows are generated using the prepayment rates forecasted using the forward rate curve. The spread is calculated by discounting each cash flow by the appropriate zero rate plus a spread. Once again that spread is varied until the discounted value equals the price of the bond. Of the three methods, the forward spread provides the best measure of value since it properly reflects the economics of the yield curve.

For each bond and for each rate environment, we will calculate a nominal spread, a zero spread and two different forward spreads, one using the ten-year model for the current coupon and another using the blended-rate model. Figure 9 provides a summary of the analysis process and the various assumptions and methods.

FIGURE 9

ANALYSIS PROCESS	SIMPLIFIED WORLD	ASSUMPTIONS
INTEREST RATES	Three Rates Determine Curve	(1) FLAT
	Zero Coupon Bonds	(2) STEEP
	No Volatility	(3) KINKED
PREPAYMENTS	Percent of Original Balance	(1) 10 year model
	Piecewise Linear-Function	(2) 1 yr/10yr model
	One Variable	
CASH FLOW	Annual Cash Flows	(1) Par Bond
	Annual Prepayments	(2) Premium Bond
	Lockout Maturity	
VALUATION	Nominal Spread	(1) Spreads
	Zero (spot) Spread	(2) Keyrate Durations
	Forward Spread	

RESULTS

Although nominal spread, that is, the yield of the bond minus the yield of the treasury with the same average life, is the most commonly used measure of value, it does not provide a consistent measure of value across different yield curve environments. To demonstrate this, we created different bonds that shared the same nominal spread and then compared their value using the other models.

For each yield curve environment (flat, steep, kinked) we created two bonds, one priced at par and one priced at 110. All six bonds have the identical structure. They all have an underlying mortgage coupon of 10.5%, a three-year lockout and a fifteen-year maturity. With this structure, the bonds would have a performance profile similar to an intermediate CMO payer created from premium collateral. The bond coupons were set so that at their base price of either par or 110, each bond would have a nominal spread of 100 basis points.

Results are shown in Figure 10. The first observation is that the bonds have different coupons. Even though the mortgage current coupon is 8%, CMO bonds with shorter average lives can be priced at par with lower coupons. It is this effect which allows CMO issuers to price some of the CMO bonds at lower yields than the collateral. This is also why, as was discussed earlier, mortgage spreads (to a point on the curve) tend to respond to the steepness of the yield curve. A steeper curve means lower yields on the early tranches. This makes CMO issuance more attractive, leading to higher collateral prices and tighter mortgage spreads.

FIGURE 10
Yield Spread Analysis

Bond/Curve	Coupon	Nominal Spread	Zero Spread	Avg. Life	Forward Spread	Ten-year Avg. Life	Forward Spread	Blended Avg. Life
Par								
Flat	8.00%	100	100	4.6	100	4.6	100	4.6
Steep	6.47%	100	90	4.6	21	8.7	21	8.7
Kinked	6.67%	100	86	4.6	51	6.0	22	7.9
Premium								
Flat	10.70%	100	100	4.6	100	4.6	100	4.6
Steep	9.06%	100	91	4.6	115	8.7	115	8.7
Kinked	9.27%	100	87	4.6	100	6.0	104	7.9

Any bond (remember we are assuming a world of zero volatility) can be represented as a sum of zero-coupon bonds. It is possible to measure the value of each bond by discounting each cash flow by the associated zero-coupon rate plus a spread. Although these bonds all have the same nominal spread, they have different zero spreads. Of course, with the flat yield curve, the discounting method doesn't matter. The bond in the steep yield curve case loses 10 basis points in spread. This loss in spread stems from two causes. First, the spread was calculated relative to the interpolated 4.0 year rather than the 4.6 year. That effect is worth about 8 basis points. The remaining 2 basis points is a result of averaging anomalies in the discount process. The wider the distribution of cash flows and the steeper the yield curve, the greater the effect.

For the kinked yield curve, the spread differential is 14 basis points due to the steepness of the front of the curve. If the bond's cash flows had extended significantly beyond the kink at the ten-year point, the nominal spread might have understated the zero spread yield due to the asymmetry of the curve and the distortion of the averaging process inherent in the nominal yield approach.

For the premium bonds, the effect on zero spread is nearly the same as for the par bonds. The zero spread will measure discrepancies in timing around the average life point. Since the timing of the cash flows of the premium bonds are nearly identical to the par bonds they exhibit nearly the same zero spreads.

When we turn to the forward-rate analysis, which is the most reliable of the three approaches, the discrepancies increase further. In the forward-rate cases, the cash flows of the bonds are calculated using the forward rates to determine the refinancing rate and the prepayment rates. The rising forward rates lead to slower prepayments, extending the cash flows, and producing longer average lives. As expected with the steep yield curve, the extended bonds have substantially lower spreads to the curve. Using the ten-year model to determine the mortgage current coupon, the spread of the par bond in the steep yield curve case declines to 21 basis points, reflecting its new average life of 8.7 years. The spread of the par bond in the kinked yield curve case declines to 51 basis points. The flatter yield curve beyond the ten-year produces higher prepayment rates than in the steep curve, and therefore a shorter average life.

Using the blended-rate model, further decreases the spread of the par bond in the kinked curve case down to 22 basis points. With the impact of rising short rates figuring into the current coupon, the average life rises from 6.0 years to 7.9 years. Due to the steepness of this part of the curve, extension of 1.9 years could cost over 40 basis points. However, since more of the cash flows are now received past the ten-year point (where the curve is flatter) the impact of extension is reduced somewhat relative to the effect anticipated from just looking at the average life.

Given the results for the par bonds, the results for the premium bonds seem to be somewhat counterintuitive. The zero spreads are as expected, but the forward spreads don't look quite right. As the bonds extend into the steep yield curve their spreads increase. This must result from the construction of the bonds. For these bonds, their coupon was set so that the price using a nominal spread of 100 basis points is 110. This results in very high coupons: 10.70%, 9.06% and 9.27% for the flat, steep and kinked cases respectively. These coupons are respectively 2.70, 3.03, and 2.60 percentage points higher than the coupons of the par bonds. These additional coupon strips are like IOs (interest only securities) added on to the original par bonds. The higher spreads in the forward rate cases reflect the positive "hedge value" of IOs in an upwardly sloping yield curve environment.

Hedge value results from the additional coupon income received when using forward rates to forecast prepayments due to the extension of the life of the security. The value of receiving roughly 300 basis points of income for several more years, more than offsets the cost of higher discount rates. For the steep curve, the effect of the higher coupon causes the zero spread to rise from 91 basis points to 115 basis points. The impact of the IO is more striking when the forward spread of 115 basis points for the premium bond is compared to the forward spread of 21 basis points for the par bond. Because of this effect, IOs can be priced at very low nominal spreads when the yield curve is steep. On the other hand, in the flat yield curve scenarios, the IO does not provide any additional hedge value. With a flat curve, the cash flows of the bond do not extend in the forward rate analysis.

The importance of forward rates on the value of the IO can be seen even more clearly in the kinked curve scenarios. Using the ten-year model of the mortgage current coupon the spread of the premium bond rises from 87 basis points to 100 basis points. This is somewhat less than the effect for the steep case. Also, the spread advantage of the premium bond is 49 basis points more than the par bond, while for the steep curve the advantage was 94 basis points. The kinked curve produces far less hedge value even though the kinked curve is actually steeper in the part of the curve where the cash flows occur. Again, the results don't seem to make sense.

This anomaly can be resolved by identifying the source of hedge value. Hedge value results from slower prepayments producing more cash flow. Slower prepayments are caused by rising refinancing rate. The projected refinancing rate is driven by the forward rate curve. For the ten-year model the forward rates are determined primarily by the ten-year rate and the thirty-year rate. The one-year rate, and hence the steepness of the front of the curve, has less impact on the mortgage current coupon forward rates. With the ten-year model a steeper back end of the curve increases hedge value. A steeper front end might decrease the hedge value through the discounting effect.

Keeping this intuition in mind as we look at the blended rate model, the results make sense. The spread for the kinked curve premium bond rises to 104 basis points. The increase is a result of the net impact of higher discount rates for longer cash flows (compare the 51 basis point spread of the par bond using the ten-year model and the 22 basis point spread for the blended rate model to get an estimate of this effect), combined with the effect of increased cash flow of the additional IO strip.

In addition to the spread analysis, it is also possible to calculate effective durations for these bonds. For this analysis we will concentrate on the flat curve scenario and the forward spreads. To calculate effective durations, we reduced the yield of the one-year, ten-year and thirty-year zeros by 25 basis points and then recalculated the value of the bond assuming a constant spread to the curve. The change in price was multiplied by four to produce a modified duration. The results shown in Figure 11 are actually *dp/dy* 's, also known as *dollar value of a basis point*. A variant on key rate durations was also calculated. These key rate durations were calculated by first reducing the thirty-year rate by 25 basis points and recalculating the bond price, then while keeping the thirty-year at the lower rate, reducing the ten-year and finally reducing the one-year rate. These calculations are a little different than the usual key rate durations because they include the effect of changing the previous rate on the next calculation.

FIGURE 11
Effective Duration Analysis

Kinked Curve		Thirty-year	Ten-year	One-year	Total
Par Bond	10yr	1.2	4.3	1.9	7.4
	2 factor	1.6	6.6	1.4	9.6
Premium	10yr	0.0	1.2	2.7	3.8
	2 factor	-0.2	1.7	2.4	3.9

Flat Curve		Thirty-year	Ten-year	One-year	Total
Par Bond	10yr	0.0	1.3	2.3	3.6
	2 factor	0.0	1.3	2.3	3.6
Premium	10yr	- 0.4	- 0.2	2.7	2.2
	2 factor	- 0.3	0.0	2.5	2.2

For the par bond, the effective duration was 3.6 years. For the premium bond the effective duration was 2.2 years. The price action of the premium bond is damped by higher prepayments producing a shorter bond and reducing the impact of lower rates on the price. It is interesting to look at the key rate durations. For the par bond, most of the change in value derives from the short end of the curve where the cash flows are concentrated. The bond shortens slightly more when the thirty-year rate is dropped using the ten-year model than when using the blended-rate model. Since the curve is flat on the part of the curve where the cash flows occur, and the bond is priced near par, shortening does not produce a change in price.

The premium bond demonstrates the same phenomenon we saw when looking at the yields. The hedge value (in this case the option value) of the bond is determined by the long end of the curve, even though all the cash flows occur on the front end. Dropping the thirty-year rate shortens the life of the security, so that the value of the premium bond falls. The effect of dropping the thirty-year is greater for the ten-year model than for the blended-rate model since the mortgage rate doesn't fall as much when the thirty-year rate is lowered when using the blended model. Because all the cash flows occur before the tenth year, varying the thirty-year only affects the timing of the cash flows. Varying the ten-year affects both the timing and discounting of the cash flows. Varying the one-year primarily affects the discounting when using the ten-year model, and affects both discounting and timing of cash flows when using the blended-rate model.

CONCLUSION

While the results in this model derive from a simplified model, the parameters were chosen so that the magnitude of the results would be comparable to actual securities. It is therefore clear that choices made in the analysis process can affect your view of value. Using standard measures of value, such as nominal yield spread, or using a prepayment model that does not adequately account for the shape of the yield curve, can lead to poor investment decisions. Moreover, analysis of mortgages is becoming more and more sophisticated so that fundamental decisions made in the modeling process are often obscured by the details.

Although this chapter does not provide an evaluation of the impact of volatility, the inclusion of volatility will generally lead to the calculation of an option cost. The option cost can be subtracted from the forward-rate spread (which is like a zero-volatility spread) to produce an option-adjusted spread (OAS). The option cost will relate primarily to the option features of the bond relative to the forward rate cash flows. This is a subtle, but important, point which would be a worthwhile topic for another paper.

Although this analysis focuses on the impact of the yield curve on MBS value with in a very simple framework, there are a number of general conclusions that can be drawn. First, the valuation technique you use is going to effect how you view the world. If you use nominal yield spreads, you are going to come up with one set of answers. If you use an option-adjusted spread or forward spreads, you are going to come up with a different point of view about relative value.

Second, the assumptions used in the modeling process can also have a large impact on the value of the security. Sometimes these assumptions are so fundamental that its not even clear that a decision has been made. For example, if you are using a one-factor interest-rate generator in an OAS model, it would seem that linking the prepayment model to one point on the curve would be sufficient. However, in doing so you ignore the impact of the shape of the forward yield curves.

Third, while this analysis may seem very theoretical, there are synthetic instruments in the market that are priced precisely off of zero curves and cash flows determined by forward rates. With mortgages, you cannot be sure whether a ten-year model or a blended-rate model is correct, or whether you need more points along the curve, or whether in certain environments prepayments are related to the curve at all. Investors looking at synthetic alternatives to CMOs and other MBS need to understand the differences between those bonds and real mortgage-backed securities. Even though there are significant differences, comparison of real and synthetic MBS can provide insight into valuation of MBS and can help set reasonable boundaries for the value of complex MBS.

CHAPTER 2

CMO YIELD ATTRIBUTION AND OPTION SPREAD

Thomas S. Y. Ho
President, Global Advanced Technology Corporation

INTRODUCTION

As the CMO market grows in size, the deals grow in complexity. Recent deals often have many bond types; PAC I, PAC II, PAC IO, floater, inverse floater, and other types of companion tranches all in the same deal. For example, FNMA 91_108 has 65 tranches and 579 pieces of collaterals (with different factors and coupons, prepaying at different speeds.) As a result, the prepayment risk of the collaterals is allocated to the different tranches in a complex fashion.

This chapter presents a relative valuation methodology: yield attribution. We show that the yield attribution approach provides a more consistent framework for analyzing a CMO tranche. In particular, we show the importance of the option spread as a significant part of the analysis. Much research has focused on the applications of OAS analysis in relative valuation and formulating portfolio strategies (see, for example, Piro (1991) and Hall (1992)). However, the research has not investigated the CMO OAS analysis; the topic that this chapter addresses.

The section on Nominal-Spread Valuation shows the use of nominal

Thomas S. Y. Ho is President of Global Advanced Technology Corporation, 40 Wall Street, New York, New York, 10005. The author would like to thank Andrew Davidson, Tom McAvity and Rhoda Woo for their many helpful comments, and Chang Liu, Robert Chang and Mark Wainger for their assistance in the research, However, he takes responsibility for any errors that may remain.

spread in identifying the value of a CMO. The section on Yield Attribution defines the yield attribution methodology. This methodology enables investors to properly identify the value of the CMO and uncover hidden risks. The section on CMO Risk Profiles presents the estimates of the option spreads of the tranches in a deal. Further, this section shows the behavior of each tranche type and the average value of each type. The conclusions are given in the final section.

NOMINAL-SPREAD VALUATION

Consider the FHLMC 1015 deal. The issued amount was $300 million, with 75% supported by mortgage pools with gross WAC 10.57%, WAM 338 months, and 9.5% pools with gross WAC 10.49% and WAM 335 months. The remaining pools have different gross WACs. The deal has 16 tranches. There are 6 PAC tranches, two supporting PACs, a PAC IO, an IO-ette, five standard companions, and a companion Z. Since the pools have different coupons, their prepayment speeds would be different, and their cash flows have to be allocated to each of the tranches according to the priority rules. Determining the present value of the cash flows of a tranche is no longer a straightforward task.

For valuing a Treasury bond, the promised payments (coupons and principals) are fixed, and the fair value is the sum of the present values of each payment discounted by the appropriate Treasury rate along the spot curve. For an option-free corporate bond, a similar procedure should apply, except that we discount the payments with an additional spread to capture the credit and liquidity risks. In the other words, the corporate bond value is determined by specifying the yield required by the term structure and the additional spread, the Option-Adjusted Spread (OAS).

Extending this approach to a CMO deal raises a number of questions. Consider the companion Z tranche of FHLMC 1015. The collateral is presently paying down at 675 PSA. The prepayment speed is at a historic high. Suppose that interest rates will not fall further in the future, and that the burnout effect on the mortgage pool will slow down the prepayment rate. Let us consider five scenarios and conduct the following "vector analysis." For each scenario, the prepayment rate falls from 600 to a lower prepayment rate after twelve months and stays constant at that rate. The five scenarios are given in Table 1 (the entries are in PSA):

TABLE 1

Scenarios	A	B	C	D	E
months 1–5	600	600	600	600	600
months 6–11	450	450	450	450	450
months 12–360	200	225	250	275	300

The results demonstrate the instability of the cash flows under the slightly different scenario assumptions. If the collateral prepayment speed stays below 250 PSA, the first payment would not be realized until 12/05, or thirteen years later. If the prepayment speed is faster than 250 PSA, then all the payments will be made within ten years. Indeed, Table 2 shows that the average life of the companion Z tranche falls from 19.11 years to 2.78 years as we assume higher prepayment speeds.

TABLE 2
FHLMC 1015: CZ 9.50 11/20 Settle date 03/06/1992

Scenarios	A	B	C	D	E
PSA after one year	200	225	250	275	300
yield at price 101–03	9.603	9.595	9.561	9.365	9.139
average life	19.11	17.78	18.40	6.15	2.78

Let us now compute the nominal spread of the companion Z tranche. Suppose the tranche price is quoted as 101-03. Given the prepayment behavior, let us assume scenario B to be most likely. For this scenario, we can derive the cash flow, as described above. With this corresponding cash flow, we can calculate the internal rate of return, called the nominal yield. The nominal yield is determined to be 9.595%. Nominal spread is the nominal yield net of the yield of the on-the-run Treasury with the closest weighted average life. Since the weighted average life of the Z tranche exceeds ten years, we can compare the yields with both the ten-year and the thirty-year bonds. The ten-year Treasury and thirty-year Treasury are trading at 7.266% and 7.811% respectively, reflecting an upward sloping yield curve. Hence the corresponding nominal yield spreads are 2.33% and 1.784%. The summary of the calculation is given in Table 3:

TABLE 3
Nominal Yield Spread
FHLMC 1015: Z 9.50 11/20

	10–year	30–year
Spread off		
Quoted Price	101-03	101-03
Nominal yield	9.595	9.595
(on-the-run)	(7.266)	(7.811)
nominal spread	2.330	1.784

The nominal yield spread suggests that the Z tranche offers an additional return, relative to the Treasury, that is between 1.784% and 2.330%. Can we make a relative valuation of the Z tranche based on this analysis?

As we know, prepayment speeds rise in step with the fall in interest rates. The investors of the Z tranche, as shown above, would receive much of the principal payments early under the low interest rates regime. When interest rates rise, the payment extends significantly ("extension risk"). This behavior is detrimental to the investors. The cost of such cash flow variations is the "option cost." The investors have to be properly compensated for such an option cost, even if the investor is risk neutral. For this reason, we must consider the nominal spread net of the option cost to correctly evaluate the additional return off the Treasury market.

There is another problem with the nominal spread. In the above example, we choose scenario B for the calculation. However, if we use scenario E, the nominal yield becomes 9.139% (see Table 2), with a change of 45.6 basis points. But the corresponding on-the-run Treasury is trading at 5.34% yield. Therefore, in this case the nominal spread is much wider. This simple example shows that the nominal spread can be very sensitive to the often ad hoc choice of the "vector." For these reasons, we present the yield attribution approach.

YIELD ATTRIBUTION

Static Yield

Yield attribution is the specification of the components of the yield of a bond. Take a callable corporate bond, for example. Given a quoted price, we can calculate the yield to maturity. But part of the yield attributes to three components: the time value of money, the call option, and the credit/liquidity spreads. Specifying the three components is the yield attribution.

A direct extension of this methodology for CMO analysis is less appropriate. Simply, the stated maturity of a CMO bears little relevance to the pricing. As in the nominal yield, mentioned above, a certain "vector" of prepayment speed is often assumed. But, we have already noted that the analytical results are sensitive to the choice of the vector. Therefore, the yield should be defined by an objective reference.

One objective and meaningful reference is the vector that is generated by assuming zero interest rate volatility. The Treasury yield curve is the benchmark for relative bond valuation. Supposing there is no interest rate uncertainty, or zero interest rate volatility, the projected future Treasury rates would be the forward rates. Using the forward rates, we can calculate the projected cash flow of the CMO (i.e. the vector for reference) via a prepayment model. The internal rate of return using this cash flow is called the static yield.

There are other possible objective references. For example, we can assume that the yield curve does not shift in the future and that all the interest rates are fixed. But this definition would confound the effects of interest rate uncertainty with the yield curve shape. The use of static yield does not require the investors to believe the forward rates to be the expected future rates. One can always calculate the nominal yield based on any vector, and compare the nominal yield to the static yield. The difference represents the divergence of your view from the zero volatility case. This difference is called the "subjective adjustment." In the special case, when the investor assumes the yield curve does not move, then the subjective adjustment is called the "hedge cost." Davidson (1992) also describes the theoretical issues of the hedge cost.

In Table 4, we summarize the discussion on the subjective adjustment.

TABLE 4

value	yield		Subjective Adjustment
price 101–03	nominal	9.595	
price 101–03	static	9.730	−0.135

Now, we continue to discuss the components of the static yields. There are three parts: yields from the spot curve (Treasury yield), the yields from the volatility (option spread), and the additional return (OAS). We derive these components from the values. The Treasury component value is relatively straightforward to derive. Since we have already calculated the cash flow under the zero volatility scenario, we can always calculate the value by the spot curve, and then the yield. The difference of the static yield and the Treasury yield is the static spread.

We can now proceed to calculate the impact of volatility on the CMO. Using a pricing model that is consistent with arbitrage-free framework (see, for example, Ho (1992)), we can calculate the CMO price and yield under the market volatility assumption and under the zero volatility assumption. The difference of the two yield values is the option spread. Finally, the difference of the static spread and the option spread is the option-adjusted spread, by definition.

We can extend Table 4 analysis further to Table 5.

TABLE 5
Yield Attributions of FHLMC 1015 CZ

TSY yield	7.098
option spread	2.040
OAS	0.592
static yield	9.730
subj. adjustment	(0.135)
nominal yield	9.595

In valuation, it is more appropriate to use the Treasury yield component than the yield of particular on-the-run issues, because the cash flow generated by the zero volatility scenario is often complex and significantly different from the principal and coupon cash flow of Treasury securities. Therefore, choosing a cash flow comparable to the on-the-run Treasury securities to decide on the appropriate yield for the cash flow can be erroneous. The mistake can be substantial particularly when the yield curve is not flat. Yield attribution approach is also particularly important for option-embedded bonds such as the CMO. Referring to Table 5, the option spread of 2.040% is significant. As a result, the additional return (OAS) on the CZ is only 59.20 basis points.

Subjective Adjustment and OAS

As noted in the discussion thus far, behind the seemingly simple idea of yield attribution is the pricing model of a CMO. The pricing model properly projects the cash flows along interest-rate paths, and discounts the cash flows, and determines the "average" price. The average price, fair value, has to be consistent in an arbitrage-free framework (as mentioned above.) The arbitrage-free condition is important. For example, suppose we have a very well-protected PAC or a VADM bond, and that we all agree that the bond has negligible embedded-option value. For this reason, we do not need to know any complex pricing model to value such cash flows. We will simply discount the cash flow along the spot curve, with a spread representing the additional return.

A pricing model for CMOs must be able to price both the option-free and option-embedded bond in one consistent fashion. Otherwise, how can we determine the option spread of a CMO tranche? Therefore, the arbitrage-free condition assures that the pricing model, using one procedure for both option-free and option-embedded bonds, can value an option-free bond consistent with the method of discounting a cash flow along the spot curve.

The arbitrage-free condition has another implication. Using the pricing model, we can simulate the CMO bond price sensitivity to all the sources of interest rate risks. Suppose we construct a Treasury portfolio that can replicate the CMO sensitivities to interest rate risks. (For example, Ho (1990) proposes a procedure using key rate durations for such a replication.) By dynamically revising this replicating portfolio of Treasuries, the portfolio returns would be similar to the CMO. There are effects outside the model, for example, the prepayments unanticipated by the model. These effects would be somewhat random. But one systematic difference between the CMO and the replicating portfolio would be that the Treasury portfolio would underperform the CMO bond by the OAS.

But when we perform a vector analysis, we are imposing our views of future interest rate movements and prepayments on the pricing of the bond. These views are often outside the context of an arbitrage-free framework. For simplicity, consider a Treasury bill. We have discussed how we would price a Treasury bill along the spot curve. But, if we conduct a total-return analysis, and impose certain interest rate scenarios, the returns will differ from the "risk-free rate." Combining vector analyses (which is based on subjective views) with the static yield (which is based on an arbitrage-free modeling framework), there will be a discrepancy. This difference is the subjective adjustment.

We use the numerical example in Table 5 to illustrate. The analysis shows that the CMO outperforms the replicating portfolio by the OAS of 59.2 basis points. But relative to the vector imposed (scenario B), the OAS return is overstated by 13.5 basis points.

Option Spread

We have shown that in yield attribution, option spread is an important part in explaining the value of a CMO. If we have some estimate of the option spread of a CMO, given a static yield, we can calculate the OAS. The importance of the option spread is that the measure is relatively insensitive to many model assumptions, as the spread represents the average of many path simulations. This section discusses the behavior of the option spreads of CMOs.

By definition, option spread is the additional expected return of the CMO which offsets the expected losses due to the prepayment risks together with interest-rate uncertainty. If there is no interest-rate risk, then the option spread is zero. For the above example, the Companion Z has to provide an additional return of over 2% every year to cover the potential loss.

The concept of the option value of a CMO tranche is best illustrated by the scattered plots of the present values of the tranche cash flow against the present values of the corresponding bond for a large sample of interest rate paths. Corresponding bond is the fixed cash flow that is generated by zero volatility and is used to calculate the static yield. Figure 1a and Figure 1b are the scatter plots of FHLMC 113E (a PAC bond) and FHLMC 113L (a PAC IO) respectively.

FIGURE 1A

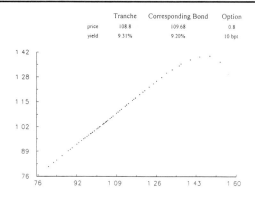

	Tranche	Corresponding Bond	Option
price	108.8	109.68	0.8
yield	9.31%	9.20%	10 bpt

FIGURE 1B

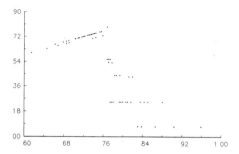

FHLMC 113E is a well-protected PAC. Using the same OAS to discount the path-dependent cash flows of the CMO and the fixed cash flow of the corresponding bond, we see that the difference is the option value of 0.8, or a spread of 10 basis points. As we can see in Figure 1a, the cash flow of the PAC is stable, and therefore the scattered plots must lie on the 45 degree line, except for some of the paths represented on the extreme right. In these cases, the PAC collars are broken, and prepayments lower the present values of the cash flows of the PAC. Note that the average value of the present values of these paths is the CMO value. Hence, the average deviations of the scattered points from the 45 degree line is the option value. We can see the option value is relatively small.

Such is not the case with FHLMC 113L, the PAC IO. The PAC IO option value is 17.52, or the option spread is 610 basis points. The scattered plots of Figure 1b depict the scenarios where the prepayments would affect the PAC IO value, resulting in a significant option value. On the right side of Figure 1b, the PAC IO is quite well protected. As a result, the plots by and large lie on the 45 degree line. But, for many falling rate scenarios where the corresponding bond has value exceeding 76, the PAC IO present values of cash flows are very low. These scenarios represent the cases in which the prepayments of the collaterals lead to significant loss of cash inflow to the PAC IO investors. Indeed, Figure 1b shows that the present values may fall below 10 in some cases.

Let us consider the option spread as a measure of risk exposure. Duration, which is the price sensitivity of a CMO to a small parallel shift of the yield curve, is another risk measure. Since the risk of the collateral is allocated across all the tranches, we would like to examine the risk sharing of the tranches relative to each other within a deal. To accomplish this analysis, we construct a scatter plot of all the tranches in a deal with the x-axis being the effective duration and y-axis the option spread. The scatter plot is called the risk profile.

Consider the risk profile of FNMA 91_39. There are eight PAC tranches, five secondary PAC tranches, a companion floater and an inverse floater and a PAC IO. The analytics are calculated as of February 25, 1992. The collateral is estimated to have effective duration of 3.5 years and option spread of 37 basis points. Referring to Figure 2, the Risk Profile of FNMA 91_39 provides interesting insights.

FIGURE 2
FNMA9139 Duration/Option Spread Plots

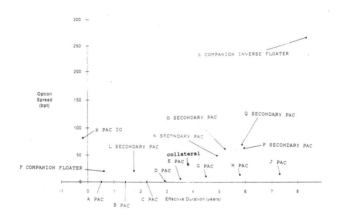

A, B and C tranches are early PACs of the deal. They are well protected from the prepayment risk. For this reason, their option spreads are zero. However, the longer PACs are less protected, particularly after recent months of high prepayment speeds. G, H, J tranches have option spreads of approximately 20 basis points.

L, N, O, P, Q are the secondary PAC tranches. They clearly have higher prepayment risks as reflected by their higher option spreads. Indeed, even though they have stated scheduled payments, the option spreads exceed 70 basis points.

F is a companion floater. As a floating rate bond, the effective duration and the option spreads are relatively low.

But, the inverse floater has risks leveraged from the floater. Therefore the S tranche has both high duration and option spread.

K is a PAC IO. As an IO, the tranche has a negative duration. Since the K tranche is not well protected, the option spread is also significant, reaching 80 basis points.

The risk profile of a deal is useful because the figure shows how the risks have been allocated. It shows the risk exposures of the secondary PACs and the PAC IO, and the risks borne by the companion tranches, particularly the inverse floater.

We should note that the risk profile depends on the robustness of the prepayment model. Both the option spread and the effective duration depends on the model assumptions. Davidson (1992), Herskovitz (1991) and others have discussed some of the issues relating to formulating a prepayment model. But, if the model understates the prepayment risk, then the understatement would affect all the tranches. As a result, the relative positions of the scatter plots of the risk profile are insensitive to the prepayment model assumptions. Hence the analysis leads to many applications.

For example, suppose we believe that the underlying collateral is going to be burnt out. That means the collateral will have lower option spread. Since all the tranche risks have to be relative to the collateral risks, we can infer quite simply the burnout effect on all the tranches. In particular, the inverse floater option-spread value should drop significantly.

CMO RISK PROFILES

While there is broad acceptance among investors that different tranche types have different risk levels in terms of embedded options, few research papers have quantified the level of the option risk. In this chapter, we consider all the agency deals, both FNMA and FHLMC, and calculate the effective duration and the option spread of all the tranches. Then we analyze the risk profile of each bond type and each tranche. There are 1033 observations. We analyze the tranches as of December 15, 1991.

Figure 3 depicts risk profiles of different bond types. Each risk profile is a scatter plot of the effective duration and the option spread of all the tranches of the agency deals belonging to the specified bond type. Refer to Figures 3a and 3b.

FIGURE 3A

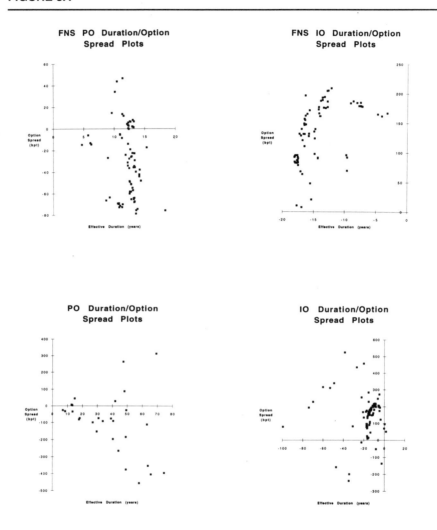

Strip IO (FNS IO)

The strip IOs have negative duration, as expected. When interest rates rise, the prepayment speed slows. Thus increasing the cash flow to the IO investors, leads to an increase in price. But the risks exposures are different depending on the coupon levels of the collateral.

When the coupon is low, say 8%, there is limited extension of the payment. Therefore, the IO does not have very negative duration. The embedded option spread is 160 basis points. For higher coupon IO, the effective duration continues to fall with the increase in option spread until the coupon reaches 9.0%. Then the duration reaches the minimal level of -17 years for a 10% coupon. Also the option spread falls. For high coupon collaterals, when interest rates rise, the IO stands to benefit significantly. Meanwhile, if interest rates fall, the further loss in IO value may be limited. Therefore, the option spread is narrowed for high coupon collaterals.

There are a few strips which have duration minus ten years and option spread of 100 basis points. They lie outside the pattern. These are the fifteen-year strips, which have less embedded option value, as one may expect. The variations of the plots forming the general pattern are the results of the different factors and WAM of the collateral of the strips.

Strip PO (FNS PO)

The collaterals are stripped to create an IO and a PO. Thus the combination of the IO and the PO is the underlying collateral. For this reason, the weighted average duration of IO and PO is that of the collateral. The option spread of the collateral should also be an approximate average of those of the IO and PO. Therefore the discussion of the risk profile of PO is similar to the IO. Referring to Figure 3a, in general, the POs have long durations, often exceeding ten-years. Also, except for the high coupon POs, the POs have negative option spreads. That means the potential gains of POs with higher prepayments outweigh the extension risk. Of course, such is not the case with high coupon strips, since the extension risks are high in these cases. The analysis shows that the POs often have high duration and negative option spreads and suggests that POs behave like call options.

IO-ettes (IO) and PO (PO)

Figure 3a is the risk profile of IO-ettes. These are the IOs within a CMO deal, and exclude the PAC IOs. Since many of these IOs (called IO-ettes) are relatively small part of the deal and often companion to the PACs, the IOs can have significant embedded options.

Referring to Figure 3a, some IO-ettes have negative duration of seventy years. That means, with a rise of 10 basis points in rates, the IO-ette can rise 7% in value. Also, some IO-ettes have option spreads exceeding 4%. That means, at an annual rate, the IO-ette has to make a return of 4% just to cover the potential loss.

Another interesting observation made in Figure 3a is that many IO-ettes do behave like the IO strips. These IO-ettes form a circular pattern in the risk profile, in a way as discussed above. This analysis shows that the behavior of many IO-ettes is comparable to the strip IOs. For this reason, arbitrage activity can assure the valuation of strip IOs and IO-ettes are relatively consistent.

For the PO analysis, we do not include the super POs. We see that the POs have very long durations, with many over forty years. Also they can have large negative option spreads. Therefore, they may have low nominal yields or static yields, but with significant potential gains.

FIGURE 3B

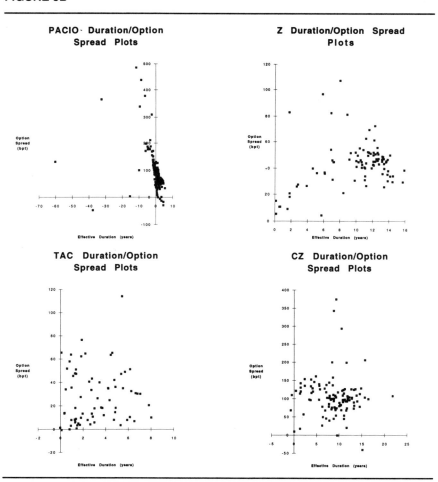

TAC (TAC)

TACs are designed to have protection of the extension risk. But the recent high prepayment speed has resulted in the TAC not being affected by the protection. This result is evident from Figure 3b. In the sample, we see that there is a wide variation of duration of TACs, ranging from zero to eight years.

Many of the TACs have significant option spreads. If we remember that collaterals have 20–35 basis point option spreads, then we can see that many TACs in fact have higher option spreads than the collateral. This is the result of the TACs being companions to the PACs. Indeed, some of the TACs have option spreads as high as 60 basis points.

Companion Z (CZ)

A Z tranche tends to have a long-stated maturity. However, a companion Z may have low duration because the experience of high prepayment rates results in early payments of the Z tranche. The effect is evident in Figure 3b.

Figure 3b shows that the effective duration of some companion Z may exceed fifteen years, but many have low duration. Indeed, some have negative duration. In these cases, the accrual rate is high and when interest rates rise, the payment would extend greatly (being a companion to PAC), and result in higher value.

Another interesting observation from Figure 3b is the significant option spread. Some companion Z tranches have option spreads exceeding 2%. The high-option spreads represent the high-risk exposure embedded in these tranches.

PAC IO (PACIO)

PAC IOs are interesting because these bonds are protected by the PAC schedule but they often have high embedded option values. Referring to Figure 3b, we see that the option spread can exceed 2%. When the schedule protection is lessened, PAC IOs often trade with a negative convexity.

PAC IOs are also companions to other PACs. For this reason, the PAC IO can have very high risk exposure. For example, Figure 3b shows that some PAC IOs can have duration below minus twenty years.

Z Tranche

When we consider the universe of Z tranches in the agency deals, we find that the results are different from those of the companion Z. For these Z tranches with no PACs in the deal, the prepayments would not shorten their duration significantly. For this reason, we see most of the Z tranches have long durations, with most of them exceeding eight years.

It is also interesting to note that the option spread by and large increases with the duration, and many Z tranches have option spread higher than 40 basis points.

Risk Profile of Tranche Types

Next, we examine the average effective duration and the average option spread value for each bond type and compare them in the risk profile. Table 6 shows the average statistics and their standard deviation of the sample. These results show us in general the risk exposure of each bond type. Figure 4 summarizes the results.

TABLE 6

		Static Yield	Effec Durat	Modif Durat	Average Life	Convexity	Option Sprd
F	avg.	8.15	2.31	6.07	10.44	2.03	-4.07
	std. dev.	0.56	2.46	2.79	6.09	4.31	21.35
IF	avg.	8.03	6.90	5.37	11.01	-6.29	143.01
	std. dev.	0.65	11.65	2.26	6.20	6.31	113.32
IO	avg.	6.65	-17.29	3.80	5.82	-3.89	141.26
	std. dev.	3.77	14.33	1.07	1.99	20.52	136.71
PAC	avg.	7.11	3.77	4.22	6.31	-0.10	6.53
	std. dev.	1.46	2.26	2.55	4.98	0.67	8.23
PO	avg.	8.00	36.50	6.35	8.81	11.67	-32.41
	std. dev.	0.82	19.82	5.24	5.95	51.65	304.38
Z	avg.	8.38	9.98	10.88	12.36	-0.64	43.26
	std. dev.	0.84	3.98	4.60	5.40	2.41	17.36
FNS PO	avg.	7.98	12.02	3.98	6.01	0.60	-31.06
	std. dev.	0.15	2.08	0.60	1.03	3.16	32.28
FNS IO	avg.	7.51	-13.91	4.02	0.07	-2.66	132.00
	std. dev	0.30	4.77	0.43	0.60	5.23	50.52

FIGURE 4

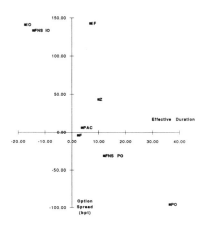

Referring to Figure 4 and Table 6 we see that, as expected, PACs have low average option spread and low standard deviation. Even though in many cases the PAC collars are broken, the embedded options may still be relatively insignificant. However, as noted above, the TAC on average has much higher option spread. The Z tranche has on average a ten-year duration and 43 basis points of option spread, higher than the collateral.

Floaters have low duration and option spreads. That means, the inverse floaters have high duration and option spreads. Indeed, the average option spread of the inverse floater is 130 basis points and the effective duration is 7.8 years. In contrast, the super floater has a negative option spread and a positive effective duration.

The average values of each tranche type do change over time. The changes reflect the level of embedded option changing with the change in interest rates as well as with the prepayments of the collateral. For example, we have seen the average option spread of TAC has increased. Noting these changes is useful. First, in managing a portfolio, it is increasingly important to manage the embedded options in the portfolio. These changes indicate how the market factors are affecting each type of bond. Second, the results can identify the riskiness of a bond relative to the average, suggesting whether the bond is unusual with "hidden risk" or not.

Option Spread and Convexity

Convexity is the second order term of the Taylor expansion of the price sensitivity with respect to a parallel shift of the yield curve (while duration is the first order term). Convexity is often used to measure the extent of the embedded option in a bond. For example, a callable corporate bond has a negative convexity because the issuer has the right to buy back the bonds at the call price. By the same argument, the passthroughs, particularly the current coupon issues, have negative convexity because the mortgagors may exercise their prepayment options. Hence, convexity and option spreads are related measures, though they have different applications. Convexity applies to total return analysis while option spread, as we discuss here, applies to yield attribution. How are they related for CMOs?

FIGURE 5A

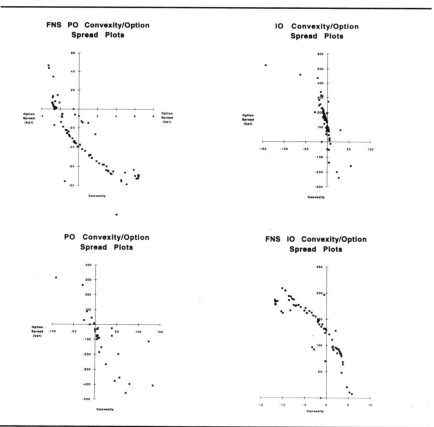

The answer depends on the bond types. Referring to Figure 5a, we see that convexity and option spreads are highly correlated for Strip IO, PO, and IO-ettes and POs. This result is quite surprising. Since convexity is a local measure (measuring the effect of a small change of interest rates on the price), one may not think that the convexity measure can capture the embedded options that are deep in or out of the money. However, convexity still captures such option effects, because the price incorporates all the option values.

However, for some other bond types, the complexity of a CMO deal often confounds the relationship between the convexity measure and the option spread with other factors. Figure 5b shows that for Z tranches and companion Z tranches, for example, the relationships no longer exist. This result shows that in a CMO, a tranche behavior near the prevailing interest rate level can be very different to its behavior when the interest rates are much higher or lower.

FIGURE 5B

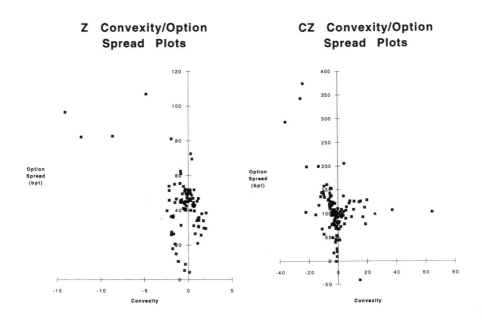

CONCLUSION

This chapter analyzes the values of CMOs. First, the chapter applies the often-used methodology "vector analysis" to yield attribution. For CMOs, this methodology is particularly important because the embedded option value can be very significant.

Next, the chapter presents estimates of the option spreads of different types of bonds. Specifically, we show how the risk of the collateral is allocated to all the tranches. The risk profile of a deal can clearly depict the effect of the allocation, enabling investors to properly identify which tranches of the deal absorb much of the risks.

The chapter then shows the behavior of each tranche type. In particular, the chapter shows that beyond the strips and PACs, all the tranche types have very diverse behavior. Some PAC may be protected in a small range of interest rate changes, but the bond may have significant embedded options, with very significant possible losses. These effects would be captured by the option spread and not necessarily the convexity.

Finally, the chapter shows how the average of the effective duration and option spread of each tranche type can be compared. These average statistics demonstrate the difference in the behavior of the bonds.

Perhaps the most important implication of the analysis in this chapter is to identify the significance of the embedded options in CMOs. While many chapters have mentioned the embedded options in CMOs, there has been no research showing how significant these options are. By identifying the option-spread level, we can conclude that the nominal spread approach in valuing a CMO can be very misleading. Indeed, the nominal spread alone cannot properly give a relative value for a CMO. The cheap/rich comparison must involve the estimate of the option spread. Valuing a CMO without using the option valuation is similar to purchasing a callable bond without taking the call provision into account. The only difference in CMOs is that the embedded-option value can be significantly higher than that of a callable bond.

REFERENCES

Davidson, Andrew, 1992, Mortgage-backed securities and the the yield curve, *Fixed-Income Portfolio Management: Issues and Solutions* (Dow Jones-Irwin, Homewood, IL), this volume pp. 1-18

Hall, Andrew, 1992, Managing mortgages against their universe–using the Fidelity OAS model, *Fixed-Income Portfolio Management: Issues and Solutions* (Dow Jones-Irwin, Homewood, IL), this volume pp. 41-57

Herskovitz, Michael, 1991, OAS and yield curve shape, Mortgage product analysis. Merrill Lynch & Co.

Ho, Thomas, 1990, Key rate durations: a measure of interest rate risks exposure, Working Paper. Salomon Brothers Center for the Study of Financial Institutions, New York University.

Ho, Thomas, 1992, Managing illiquid assets and linear path space, *Journal of Fixed Income* (forthcoming).

Piros, Christopher, 1991, On the validity of option-adjusted spreads as measures of relative value, Massachusetts Financial Services.

CHAPTER 3

MANAGING MORTGAGES AGAINST THEIR UNIVERSE: *USING THE FIDELITY OAS MODEL*

Andrew Hall
Director of Quantitative Research, Fidelity Investments

INTRODUCTION

Mortgage pricing models are widely used for trading and portfolio management. These models consist of several parts: a) interest-rate generation process b) prepayment modeling and c) mortgage-backed security (MBS) specifications. Collectively, these types of mortgage models are often referred to as option-adjusted spread (OAS) models.

Despite the prevalent use of the OAS models for mortgage-backed securities valuation, few papers to date have investigated the effectiveness of the models. While one Wall Street securities firm has shown evidence of the trading applications of the models, little research has systematically documented the usefulness of the models from the point of view of managing a mortgage portfolio.

The purpose of this chapter is to explain relative value in mortgages and the risks that they have relative to an MBS index. We want to try to identify which strategies have worked well historically and which ones are most likely to work well in the future. As a side issue, which is mostly relevant to mutual funds, this chapter shows that managing a fund for SEC yield, which is a biased measure of value, is not appropriate from an empirical point of view.

Andrew Hall is Director of Quantitative Research, Fidelity Investments, Fidelity Management and Research Company, 1 Boston Place, 40th Floor, Boston, Massachusetts, 02109.

The first section will describe the data and the second section will describe the basic analytical framework. The third section will discuss the empirical tests conducted for this chapter. The results are reported in the fourth section. One of the main results of the study is that the OAS model can indeed determine relative value. The mortgage markets have become increasingly efficient in recent years. The fifth section will describe some of the tests of portfolio strategies and the last section contains summary remarks.

DESCRIPTION OF THE DATA

For the empirical analysis, we examine monthly data going from the beginning of 1986 through the end of April 1991. The data is on actively traded issues only. The data consists of prices of thirty-year and fifteen-year passthroughs, their market values (to calculate the index weights), the last SMM (to calculate SEC yield), holding period SMM (to calculate total return) and, of course, the WAC and WAM of the issues.

For this study, only the thirty-year mortgages were included. The fifteen-year mortgages were excluded because the Fidelity fifteen-year prepayment models had not yet been written. The fifteen-year mortgages currently comprise about 10% of the index, perhaps rising to 20% by year end.

The following calculations were performed on the data: one month actual total returns; OAS; option-adjusted duration and convexity; projected total returns on seven scenarios; the SEC yield; and the differential total return which is the total return on the mortgage minus the total return on an equivalent duration Treasury barbell. Understanding the determinants of differential return is a large part of the art of running mortgage money. The Treasury barbell chosen was a simple one — the two on-the-run Treasuries that straddled the option-adjusted duration of the mortgage. We might have achieved a better match if we had picked a basket of Treasuries that more closely matched the distribution of cash flows we expect to get from the mortgage.

ANALYTICAL BACKGROUND

Three separate indices were studied. The first index is comprised of all the thirty-year mortgages that were priced. The second index was GNMAs only, because we have several GNMA funds. For the third index, we have created a short duration (2.5 year) MBS index which was constructed by adding passthroughs, one by one, starting with the lowest durations until the aggregate duration of the index reached the 2.5 year target. This probably is not the optimal way to have a short duration mortgage index. Such an index would most likely include some longer issues, some IOs, some short CMOs, some super floaters, and some ARMs. Since we do not have a reliable price history on these sectors, these instruments were not included in this study. For each index, the monthly total returns of each index and their cumulative total returns were calculated.

FIGURE 1
Lehman MBS Index vs. MBS Thirty-Year Index
Cumulative Total Return and Difference

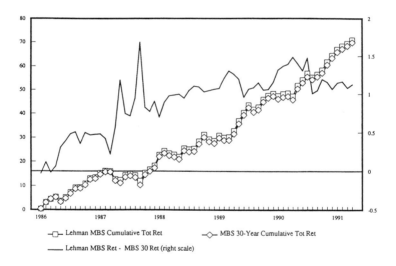

- Cumulative returns differ by only 1.1% over 64 months.

To see how these indices resemble what we have seen in the public indices, consider Figure 1, which graphs the cumulative total return of the Lehman MBS and our MBS thirty-year index. The Lehman index is indicated by square markers while the diamonds are our MBS thirty-year index; they are virtually on top of each other. The cumulative returns are measured on the left-hand scale. They go up to a total return of around 70% over the sixty-four months studied. The solid line, measured on the right-hand scale illustrates the difference between the two cumulative returns. It peaks out at about 1.7% and ends up around 1.1%. If we annualize that cumulative difference, it comes out to about 14 basis points a year. The two indices are really very much the same.

FIGURE 2
Lehman GNMA Index vs. GNMA Thirty-Year Index
Cumulative Total Return and Difference

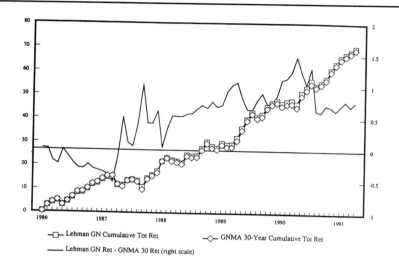

—□— Lehman GN Cumulative Tot Ret   —◇— GNMA 30-Year Cumulative Tot Ret

—— Lehman GN Ret - GNMA 30 Ret (right scale)

• Cumulative returns differ only 0.8% over 64 months.

Figure 2 shows the same results for the GNMAs. Those indices were even closer, the difference is 80 basis points over sixty-four months, which is about 8 basis points a year after accounting for compounding.

At this point, a discussion of the methodology used in calculating the OASs is in order. A Monte Carlo technique is employed. Two interest rates are used in the simulation; the one-month bill rate and the ten-year Treasury. OASs are calculated using historical yield volatilities, looking back five years for both the one-month and the ten-year. A correlation of 93% was assumed between the long and short rates. A 25 basis point shift was used for shocking the yield curve up and down in order to get the duration and convexity estimates.

The rate process is a mean-reverting lognormal-based process with arbitrage-free conditions imposed. It prices Treasuries properly and if the process is used to calculate European put and call prices on Treasuries, put-call parity is assured. It has the basic arbitrage properties that we expect. We use the current version of the Fidelity mortgage prepayment models which are in the process of being updated. Right now the inputs are relative coupon, age, and a rather complex, filtered rate history that captures both the seasoning and burnout, and, of course, the month of the year. There are no explicit housing variables in the model currently, but we will be adding a "housing turnover" variable soon. That should increase the predictive power of the model in extreme housing markets.

EMPIRICAL TESTS

The first empirical test is a cross-sectional study that takes these monthly observations and lumps them all together in one big bucket. This resulted in over 5300 observations. This is a somewhat naive test in that we are not correcting for the scale of OAS at different points in time. For example, the average market OAS may be at 50 basis points (bp) at one time and at 100 bp another. In other words, it measures value across all times in the study, not in the available universe of investments at one time.

Another constraint on the test is that we are only studying one-month total returns. In order to have the OAS predicting differential returns well, the market has to correct mispricings within a very short time frame. Frequently, during the time period of the test, mispricings of issues in the MBS market persisted for several months.

The cross-sectional method is similar to that used at Morgan Stanley. All 5310 observations were ranked by different variables and then the bucket results were averaged for a cross-sectional study. Next, we threw a statistical model at the data, which gave quite interesting results. Unfortunately, the monthly data is too noisy for a direct application of the statistical results.

In the second part of the study, we tried to pick "optimal" portfolios at the beginning of each month. This is no longer a cross-sectional study, it is now a time-series study. This mirrors what we, as money managers, want to do from month to month, from day to day, in the portfolios we actually manage. Given the universe of potential investments today, how should we structure our portfolios to have the highest expected return? The main purpose of this study is to try to find out how to optimize the portfolio, how to select a portfolio with the highest expected return. By studying various strategies we hope to discover good techniques. Presented here are a couple of fairly simple strategies. We will try to relate some of the under and outperformance of these portfolios to market conditions.

In the cross-sectional study, the 5310 observations are ranked by one variable at a time, and then quartile and deciles relative to the chosen variable are calculated. For example, we tried to see if the highest OAS bucket predicted the highest differential return with a high frequency of outperformance. As mentioned previously, this study was quite handicapped because we only had one-month returns here and it often takes the market more than one month to recognize a MBS mispricing.

EMPIRICAL RESULTS

At the top of Figure 3, we have OAS quartiles. For example, if we took the top quarter of those 5310 observations in OAS, we had an average OAS of 119 basis points and an average SEC yield spread (the SEC yield of the mortgage minus the yield on its duration equivalent Treasury) of 178 basis points. The third column is how much the OAS changed, in this case a tightening of 5 basis points over one month. The fourth column shows how frequently the MBS outperformed the duration matched Treasury (71% of the time), and finally, the last column indicates what the magnitude of monthly outperformance was (33 bp). If we compound this monthly excess return on top of the base line returns we would get a much bigger number, 6% a year or so of annual outperformance. Of course, many of the top performers in the top bucket may be from the same time period, and the best opportunities were not available each month.

FIGURE 3
OAS Quartile and Decile Results

Quartiles by OAS				
OAS	SEC Yld Spread	Delta OAS	Pct of Times Outperforming	Differential Return
119	178	-5	71	33
67	145	-1	66	15
53	140	2	63	4
35	148	5	53	-8

	Deciles by OAS			
OAS	SEC Yld Spread	Delta OAS	Pct of Times Outperforming	Differential Return
169	198	-6	70	34
90	166	-5	72	34
75	156	-2	68	24
68	147	-2	71	20
63	138	1	60	7
58	138	2	65	3
52	139	1	64	8
46	139	2	63	2
40	146	4	53	-3
25	157	8	46	-17

• The OAS Model was a very good indicator of value over the period studied.

Figure 3 shows that the OAS model performed quite well as an indicator of value. The highest OAS bucket had the highest differential return, the highest percentage of outperforming and it predicted a 5 basis point tightening over just one month. The next lower bucket was not as good, it tightened by just 1 basis point and outperformed by 15 basis points a month. Taking a closer look, the decile table again shows the desired monotonic behavior. The OAS model did identify value quite accurately over time.

This is actually a simultaneous test of the OAS as an indicator of value and the option-adjusted duration as a measure of interest rate risk. If we had a very biased estimate of duration, we would have had a lot more noise in the differential return column. We would also notice differential performance between bull and bear markets — behavior that was not observed in the data.

The same test was repeated with the SEC yield spread in Figure 4. It performed reasonably well. In this measurement, it appears as if the SEC yield performed about 2/3 as well as the OAS as an indicator of value, but we will see later that SEC yield only performed about 1/2 as well as the OAS when used in a more realistic test. We added another column of results to this table. In the far right column is the average price of the bucket, which shows the distinct bias of the SEC yield measure towards the higher coupon issues. The average prices were tested for bias in the OAS-based buckets, and no bias was detected.

FIGURE 4
SEC Quartiles and Decile Results

Quartiles by SEC Yld Spread					
OAS	SEC Yld Spread	Delta OAS	Pct of Times Outperforming	Differential Return	Ave Price
83	233	-2	71	26	103.21
65	165	-1	66	15	100.30
63	131	1	60	7	97.47
64	80	3	56	-3	95.39

Deciles by SEC Yld Spread					
OAS	SEC Yld Spread	Delta OAS	Pct of Times Outperforming	Differential Return	Ave Price
99	275	-4	74	35	104.05
73	212	-2	69	22	103.16
69	186	0	67	17	101.39
65	168	0	68	13	100.48
63	154	-1	65	15	99.70
61	141	0	62	10	98.35
62	129	2	58	4	97.11
66	114	2	61	3	96.31
62	96	2	60	2	94.74
66	48	4	50	-10	95.64

• The SEC yield spread was a good indicator of value, but not as good as OAS.
• Note the average price bias of SEC yield spread, no such pattern emerged for the OAS ranking.

Finally, the observations are ranked by differential return — the hindsight method. Of course, this is impossible to do in the market because no one knows the total return in advance. It is interesting to see the characteristics of the other variables in the best performing buckets. Naturally, we have high OASs in these high buckets. We have enormous reversion of OAS, with an average tightening of 26 basis points.

FIGURE 5
Differential Return Decile Results
(Hindsight)

Deciles by Differential Return					
OAS	SEC Yld Spread	Delta OAS	Pct of Times Outperforming	Differential Return	Delta Ten-Year
110	186	-26	100	114	16
73	156	-11	100	62	5
68	152	-8	100	47	6
65	148	-5	100	36	3
60	148	-4	100	25	3
61	152	0	100	12	2
56	151	3	32	-2	-5
58	141	7	0	-21	-10
65	142	15	0	-45	-17
72	146	33	0	-115	-24

• Note the rate directionality of the return buckets. When mortgages outperform — rates go up (or vice versa.)

Perhaps the most interesting result can be seen the last column, the change in the ten-year rate. When the ten-year yield goes up, mortgages tighten and outperform strongly. When the ten-year goes down, the mortgages widen and perform poorly. It is important to be aware of the mortgage spread change patterns; these should be built into projected total returns. Prepayment fears rise as rates drop causing spreads to widen and, conversely, as rates rise, price compression unwinds and people forget about prepayment risk allowing MBS OASs to tighten. As recently as one and a half years ago, people were saying mortgages will never again hit the 1986-87 prepayment peaks. However, we are now experiencing prepayments close to that historical level and are expected to surpass the previous peaks in April or May. We calculated the correlation matrix of a few of the variables in the cross-sectional study. The results are given in Figure 6. Remember, these are one-month total returns and the data is very noisy. The selected variables are differential return, the ten-year Treasury, the OAS, the SEC yield spread, the change in OAS which has the most explanatory power, as it very well should. (If the change in OAS does not explain most of the differential return then there is something seriously wrong with the OAS model).

FIGURE 6
Cross-Sectional Statistical Results

Regression Results [Unweighted]

Variable	Parameter Estimate	Standard Error	Signif Level
CONST	0.9056	0.1722	0.999
TenYr	-0.1384	0.1841	0.999
OAS	0.0149	0.0023	0.999
SECSpr	0.0712	0.0153	0.999
Slope	0.0004	0.0002	0.956
Vol90D	0.0083	0.0017	0.999

- The sample period was generally one of falling Treasury yields and tightening MBS spreads, but around that trend, the ten-year Treasury and OAS (or SEC yield spread) tended to move in opposite directions.
- Not surprisingly, changes in OAS tend to explain most of the observed total return spread over Treasuries.

The slope of the yield curve is defined as the ten-year yield minus the two-year yield, the volatility used is the ninety-day historical Eurodollar volatility. All these variables are significant, but the fit is very poor. It would also be interesting to apply other techniques such as using a longer total return period; normalizing for the current OAS level; or using the OAS minus the six-month average OAS as the indicator of value.

FIGURE 7
Cross-Sectional Statistical Results
Regression of Beginning-of-Month Variables of DiffRet

Correlation Analysis [N = 5310]

	DiffRet	TenYr	OAS	SECSpr	ΔOAS	Slope	Vol90D
DiffRet	1.000						
TenYr	-0.211	1.000					
OAS	0.186	-0.455	1.000				
SECSpr	0.152	-0.420	0.194	1.000			
ΔOAS	-0.885	0.158	-0.186	-0.074	1.000		
Slope	0.096	-0.229	0.097	0.162	-0.057	1.000	
Vol90D	0.123	-0.105	0.229	0.139	-0.099	0.259	1.000

N= 5310; R^2= 0.071; No other variables significant at 85% level
- TenYr is acting as a crude proxy for MBS/Treasury spread level: on average, higher long rates correlate with tighter spreads, lower excess returns.
- Adjusted for rate levels, OAS and SECpr both served as predictors of next month's return spread, but one-month relationship is very noisy.

We also attempted to build a regression model using these same variables to try to explain the differential return. These parameters came in with their estimates and their standard errors. The results show that they are very significant; the slope is the only variable with a significance level of less than .999. As previously stated, the explanatory power is low; the R^2 is just .07. The signs of the variables are interesting. The ten-year shows up with a negative sign because it is the ten-year at the beginning of the month. If the beginning ten-year is high then we probably expect it to drop over the month and spreads to widen. When we investigate these issues on a deeper level, some of these techniques could be quite interesting to try to help drive the total return calculator that is used to optimize the portfolio.

Figure 1 shows the constraints used in the optimizations. We invest the whole portfolio in mortgages, with no cash or Treasury option. The duration is equal to that of the index. The convexity is greater than the index convexity times .85. So if the index convexity is $(-100)^2$ years, the portfolio will have convexity better than $(-85)^2$ years. To handle the liquidity problems of the mortgages and to constrain the portfolio away from buying all GNMAs 16s in the middle of 1987 when there were a limited number of them, constraints on how much the portfolio could hold of each issue, based on what percentage of the index's market value each issue represented are used. If the issue was between 0 and 1% of the index, the portfolio could hold three times the issue's index weight. In other words, if some small issue that is only 1/2 of 1% of the index, the portfolio is allowed to hold 1.5% of the portfolio in that issue. Similarly, if it is between 1 and 2, the portfolio can hold four times; if it is in between 2 and 3, the portfolio can hold five times, and in between 3 and 100%, the portfolio can hold seven times.

In further study, we might have the procedure to know what the portfolio owns and know what the cost to trade any issue (bid/ask spread). We would have to estimate the bid/ask spread based on the size of the trade. It is easy to go out and buy $1 or $2 million GNMA 13s. If we go out and try to buy 100 million, we move the price at least a point. The model would have to be fairly intelligent to set the transaction cost as a function of the size of the issue, the size of the outstanding float of that issue and the size of the trade that we want to do.

OPTIMIZED PORTFOLIO PERFORMANCE

Below is a series of graphs where we study an optimal portfolio, optimized with respect to some variable or the other, versus an index. These portfolios hold four to ten issues each month. The portfolio has turnover of 100% in couple of months to more like 25-50% in other months. Let us describe the first one in Figure 8 carefully. This is the whole MBS thirty-year index and we have optimized just on the raw OAS. There is no correction for any differences in scale between the GNMA model and the FNMA model and the Freddie model shown here. Later, we will to try to see if our model reveals a systematic scale difference. The scale was about 15 to 20 basis points lower for GNMAs.

FIGURE 8
Optimal OAS MBS Portfolio vs. MBS Index
Cumulative Total Return and Difference

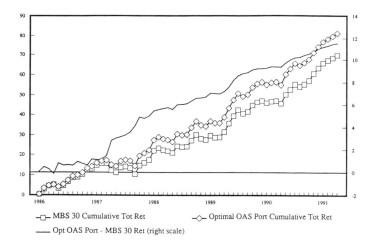

- Optimized portfolio beats index by 11.53% over 64 months.
- The annualized outperformance was 137 bp/year.

A problem Ho (1992) is solving with Linear Path Space is evaluating all option values based on the same interest rate model and the same prepayment models. This is important when we are trying to compare OASs on corporates to mortgages. People normally use a binomial model for corporates and a Monte Carlo for MBSs and the scales may be totally unrelated. One simple way to correct for scale differences is to use the option model to project a total return where we have an OAS constant or an appropriate change in the OAS. This cancels out the scale difference. The model used here does not correct for scale although the results would be better if it did.

The squares in Figure 8 indicate the MBS thirty-year index cumulative return. The diamonds represent the optimal OAS models' cumulative return. Those are both measured on the left scale. The solid line going up towards the right is the difference between the two, measured on the right-hand scale. The portfolio outperformed over the sixty-four month period by 11.5%, which is about 137 basis points a year.

FIGURE 9
Optimal OAS MBS Portfolio vs. MBS Index
Twelve-Month Moving Average Total Returns

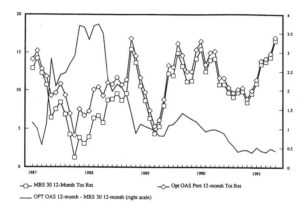

- Optimized portfolio beats index more in 1987-1989, outperformance has been between 50 and 100 bp/year since 1989.

Figure 9 shows that the results are not as good now as they were before. This is the same data comparing the same elements, except each point is the trailing twelve-month cumulative total return. The graph begins with 1987 because that was the first point at which we had a full twelve months. The two curves, the index total return and the optimal OAS total return, track each other quite closely. The optimized portfolio surpasses the index. If we considered the cumulative returns, we were winning by almost 4% per annum in the 1987-88 region and that has come down to around 100 in the 1989-90 era, and now for the last year or so we have been levelling at 50 basis points of excess return. It now appears that by using raw OAS, we cannot attain much excess returns.

Further, instead of optimizing on OAS, we optimized on total return — another hindsight version. Over the whole period of time, the optimized portfolio outperformed the index by 36%. This is perfect foresight. We use the same constraints, but we select the portfolios with the highest total returns. In the beginning period, 1986, when the OAS strategy was winning by 3.5% a year, the highest possible outperformance was 7.2%. In the last year, the best portfolio had an outperformance of 1.2%. This means that if we had perfect foresight right now and all we could play with was passthroughs, we could only beat the index by about 100 basis points. The OAS model is doing just as well now as it was then; it was providing about half of the possible outperformance in 1986-87, and now it is providing about 50 basis points compared to 100 basis points in 1986-87. We conclude from these result, that the mortgage market is getting too efficient. Thus, we have to look at some of the more exotic derivatives and analyze them very carefully in order to be able to get a more significant edge.

The market now has increased efficiency because general knowledge levels are higher. In the past, traders tended not to look at the fundamental long-term values. Instead, they looked at short-term technicals; what was being traded and by whom. Because of this, it is the research departments from Wall Street and the researchers that are developing models on the buy side that help make the market more efficient. The models tend to agree. Our edge will come from going into derivatives and having a superior model.

Another possible explanation is that the model was able to beat the market in more volatile times. Perhaps the lower excess returns recently available are due to more to reduced volatility than to increased knowledge. The market gets less efficient in volatile periods. There were also big prepayment events going on in the profitable periods. The passthrough market has shown efficiency through the latest prepayment event, which rivals the one in 1986-87. However value in derivatives has swung around a lot. For this study, we spent a lot of time reviewing levered prepay bets. The derivative markets have over-reacted quite a bit and gone back and forth a couple of times in the last two years between IOs and POs being radically over and undervalued.

The conclusion that can be drawn from Figure 10 is that the OAS has predicted three and four-month returns a lot better than it predicted one-month returns. The pluses that are scattered all on the graph are the one-month returns. The filtered, longer-term returns are the hollow squares. The solid squares are the returns predicted by the model.

FIGURE 10
Timeseries Study of OAS Optimal Portfolio
December 1985-March 1991

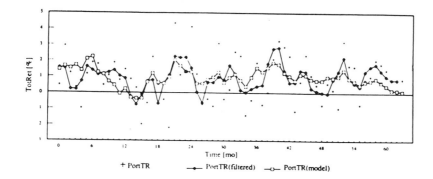

+ PortTR   ——●—— PortTR(filtered)   —○— PortTR(model)

- Construct the OAS-optimal portfolio holding each month, and attempt to predict its one-month-ahead total return from a simple linear model using OAS and SEC Yld.
- If we filter the independent noise process out of the return series, the fit of the simple model rises markedly.
- This is equivalent to saying that OAS is a better predictor of 3- to 6-month total returns.

Figure 11 uses optimal SEC yield portfolios. The SEC yield optimal portfolios outperformed by 5%, not the 11% the optimal OAS portfolios returned.

FIGURE 11
Optimal OAS MBS Portfolio vs. Optimal SEC Yld MBS Portfolio
Cumulative Total Return and Difference

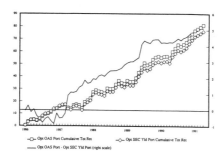

—□— Opt OAS Port Cumulative Tot Ret   —○— Opt SEC Yld Port Cumulative Tot Ret
—— Opt OAS Port - Opt SEC Yld Port (right scale)

- Optimized OAS portfolio beats optimized SEC yield by 5.13% over 64 months.
- The annualized outperformance was 60 bp/year.

In doing the same study with the GNMA index, the "optimal" portfolios outperformed their index by 9.4%. It is not surprising that the GNMA results were a little worse than the general MBS results. The GNMA market has been more efficient for a long time.

FIGURE 12
Optimal OAS GNMA Portfolio vs. GNMA Index
Cumulative Total Return and Difference

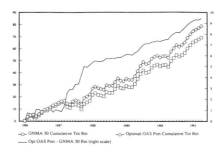

- Optimized portfolio beats index by 9.43% over 64 months.
- The annualized outperformance was 113 bp/year.

Figure 13 shows the SEC yield formula measured value better in GNMAs than it did in the conventionals, again a comment on the relative efficiencies of these markets.

FIGURE 13
Optimal OAS GNMA Portfolio vs. Optimal SEC Yld GNMA Portfolio
Cumulative Total Return and Difference

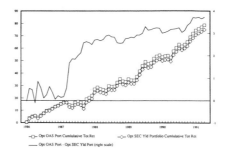

- Optimized OAS portfolio beats optimized SEC yield by 3.72% over 64 months.
- The annualized outperformance was 44 bp/year.

Finally, Figure 14 shows that the total returns were quite a bit lower for the short MBS index because they were shorter bonds and we had declining rates over this period of time. But the outperformance was on the same magnitude, about 9.3%, which is 116 basis points per year.

FIGURE 14
Optimal OAS Short MBS Portfolio vs. Short MBS Index
Cumulative Total Return and Difference

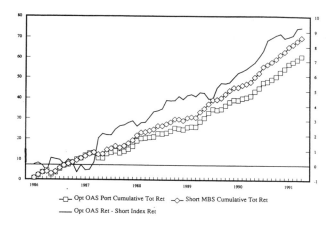

—□— Opt OAS Port Cumulative Tot Ret   —◇— Short MBS Cumulative Tot Ret
——— Opt OAS Ret - Short Index Ret

- Optimized OAS short MBS portfolio beats short MBS index by 9.26% over 64 months.
- The annualized outperformance was 116 bp/year.

CONCLUSION

What is the best way to implement mortgage strategies? Should you use an OAS-based rule? A candidate for value indicator is projected total return based on a work out OAS reverting towards either the long-term mean or towards the average of their sector.

Our project here was to establish a historical framework in which to evaluate mortgage strategies. The strategies we used outperformed quite significantly, providing about one half of what was possible across time. We hope that more sophisticated strategies and a move towards derivatives will provide significant excess returns for the portfolios for a long time.

CHAPTER 4

ILLIQUID SECURITIES: *ISSUES OF PRICING AND PERFORMANCE MEASUREMENT*

Duen-Li Kao
Director, Investment Research,
General Motors Investment Management Corporation

INTRODUCTION

Illiquid securities, as the adjective implies, normally exhibit little or no trading activity in the secondary markets. Notwithstanding, they constitute a large and integrated part of U.S. capital markets. Examples of these securities include letter stocks, private debt or convertible securities, bank loans, guaranteed insurance contracts, limited partnerships, real estate and commercial mortgages. They provide an important avenue for raising capital and investing assets. Traditional participants of illiquid security markets are banks and insurance companies. U.S. pension funds with their increasing influence on capital markets and the economy over the last decade, are also becoming significant players in this market segment.

Citing the complexity of security structure and the lack of reliable databases, market participants largely ignore most analytical techniques of security valuation used in pricing publicly traded securities. Consequently, illiquid securities are traditionally carried at cost or at highly subjective "market" values. Risk and return profiles of these instruments and their

Duen-Li Kao is Director, Investment Research, General Motors Investment Management Corporation, 767 Fifth Avenue, New York, New York, 10153. The author would like to thank Drs. Jari Kallberg and Tom Ho for their comments and criticisms.

roles in the institutional asset/liability management practices remain vague. The recently proposed FASB No. 107, so-called market-to-market valuation accounting, has generated heated debate about its appropriateness in terms of accounting disclosure (e.g., Hempel and Simonson (1992); Morris (1992)). Nevertheless, the proposal properly addresses the need for a comprehensive disclosure of the security's fair value.

Ideally, an objective security pricing framework should provide lenders and investors with the means to:

1. adequately measure asset value and performance,

2. serve as an objective basis for performance fee structure,

3. employ an analytical approach to asset/liability management,

4. obtain a reference price for security issuance, and

5. comply with regulatory disclosure requirements.

The following sections present an analytical framework for objectively valuing and monitoring the performance of illiquid securities. The discussions emphasize issues applicable to private debt and commercial mortgages. Specifically, a practical solution to developing performance benchmarks for commercial mortgage investments is presented.

EXISTING PRICING APPROACHES

In pricing illiquid securities, one common method is matrix pricing. The methodology is derived from the seminal research by Fisher (1959), which examined the linear relationship between the yield spread of a security over Treasury and various microeconomic common factors such as earnings, leverage and marketability. The essence of this method can be easily applied to instruments in different debt markets by relating yield spread to a set of external factors. The outcomes from this model are the risk premiums attributable to these factors.

As discussed in Ho (1990), the matrix pricing approach cannot accurately value a security since the resulting yield and yield components are static measures and do not take into account the dynamic nature of the changes in interest rate levels, volatilities and other pricing components. Moreover, to make this approach meaningful in pricing private securities, the model has to build upon a large database with detailed information about the security and the characteristics of the issuer.

As an alternative, one can use standard term structure theories and option pricing models to price illiquid securities. Like public fixed-income securities, the yield of an illiquid instrument is comprised of the following components: Treasury yield with comparable maturity (or duration), economic/industry sector risk, quality rating risk, option value and security risk specifically related to the creditworthiness of the company or under-lying collateral. Practitioners in the illiquid asset investment community often poll internal and external expert opinions to subjectively identify yield components related to sector, quality rating and options.

In addition, illiquid securities demand certain yield premiums unrelated to credit risk over comparable publicly traded counterparts.[1] Non-credit yield premium is attributable to (1) lower liquidity from the investor's inability to trade the securities freely, (2) lower flotation costs vis-à-vis public offerings, and (3) potential savings from direct contact and negotiation between lenders and borrowers (Zwick (1980)). For a *newly* issued private market security, additional yield differential between issuing in private versus public markets may also come from (1) potential imbalance of credit supply and demand in the markets, and (2) the time lag relationship between private commitment rates and public bond rates.

Obviously, there are numerous data on corporate bond markets that can be modified for the purpose of pricing illiquid assets. Blackwell and Kidwell (1988) revealed that the motive of issuing securities in private vis-à-vis public markets is to minimize the *overall* costs—flotation costs, agency costs and capital market search costs. Thus, the application of public bond market information to the pricing of private debt requires careful examination of the firm's characteristics related to both credit and non-credit risks. If an issuer of private securities has outstanding public debt, the pricing becomes less problematic. However, this requires the investors to identify and isolate yield premiums based on differences between private and public securities in liquidity, rating, seniority, structure, debt covenants and option-like characteristics.

If there is no public debt from the same issuer, the analyst has to find one or more public securities with comparable credit characteristics on an option-adjusted basis. To solve this matching problem, it requires a credit risk assessment model similar to those implied in the rating process. Even if a perfect credit model was available, the matching approach is hardly a final solution, especially for securities in the comparable rating range of BBB or lower. Particularly, the terms of many private securities differ greatly. As well, quoted yields of public bonds with similar "quality ratings" or of bonds in the same economic sector can be quite diverse.

DEFAULT-BASED PRICING APPROACH

Since a credit evaluation model is the essential part of the process of pricing an illiquid security, an alternative to existing security pricing approaches is to incorporate credit risk elements directly into the pricing model. A certainty equivalent model (CEM) proposed by Silver (1973) can serve such a purpose. The fundamental concept of a CEM is rather simple. It reverses the risk adjustment in the present value calculation through a certainty equivalent factor. Traditionally, the price of a debt obligation is the sum of the *promised or contractual* cash flows discounted at a risk-adjusted yield (default-free rate plus risk-bearing yield premium). If each promised cash flow is adjusted for its uncertainty, it becomes the equivalent risk-free cash flow. Thus, the discount rate used under such a framework is the risk-free rate. Mathematically, the present value function is transformed from:

$$P= \sum_{i=1}^{N} \frac{C_i}{(1+y_i)^i} \quad \text{into} \quad \sum_{i=1}^{N} \frac{C_i * A_i}{(1+r_i)^i}$$

where P is the debt's market price; C_i is the promised cash flow (coupon, principal or any prepayments) in the ith period in the future (i=1,2,...,N); A_i is the default adjustment factor (or certainty coefficient) and $A_i < 1$ ($A_i=1$ for default-free bonds); y_i and r_i are the risk-adjusted and default-free yields respectively.

This default-based pricing model was employed by Bierman and Hass (1975) to explain the cost of debt capital and the firm's debt capacity. Yawitz (1977) extended the model to consider the terms of settlement in the event of default—salvage or recovery value. Rodriguez (1985) and Yawitz et al. (1985) generalized the model by relaxing the tax-free assumption. The former used the model to examine the dependence of yield spreads on the remaining life of the security. Ho (1990) applied the default risk framework to value corporate debt obligations and to study the relationship between default probabilities and option-adjusted yields of corporate bonds.

In short, the default adjustment factor (A_i) is jointly determined by default probabilities and salvage rate. Thus, the adjusted cash flow ($C_i * A_i$) is the sum of the following two components: (1) the promised cash flow (C_i) with a probability of $P_{(0,t)}$, where $P_{(0,t)}$ is the cumulative survival probability from time 0 to time t; and (2) the *present value* of cash flow at the default settlement with a probability of $P_{(0,t-1)} * (1-P_{(t-1,t)})$. (Cash flow at the default settlement is defined as the sum of the promised coupon payments omitted and final principal payments multiplied by salvage rate.) As a result, two bonds with the same yield spreads (risk differentials) need not have the same default probabilities. This implies that an issuer with a higher expected default probability can borrow at the same rate if it increases the expected recovery rate by increasing the collateral require-ment or by purchasing credit insurance.

Furthermore, due to the nonlinear nature of yield calculation, the shape of yield curve also influences the relative default probabilities of bonds for different terms to maturity. That is, a *constant* credit yield spread across all the maturity range under the traditional yield spread framework assumes a constant risk differential. However, the default risk based model may indicate different risk premiums depending on the shape of the yield curve. In fact, a rising yield curve implies a flatter curve of default rates across maturity than an inverted yield curve.

It should be noted that for an illiquid security, the discount function in the above equation is the risk-free rate plus the illiquidity premium (or adjustment unrelated to credit risk as discussed in the section above, *Existing Pricing Approaches*). Finally, since the equation simply rearranges how risk adjustment should be made, it does not change the foundation of how an option is valued. Thus, it can be easily incorporated into standard term structure and option pricing models.

DEFAULT PROBABILITIES

In the studies mentioned in the previous section, the *conditional* default probability is assumed to be independent of the length of time of survival. That is, the probability of default in the next period given that the firm has survived up to that point is constant; i.e., $P_{(t,t+n)} = P^n$ where P is the one-period survival probability and n is the unit of time in the future from time t. Obviously, the assumption of constant or time-dependent conditional default probabilities has a significant influence on security pricing. This is similar to how constant yield and term-dependent spot rates may result in different bond values or option values.

Default Probability: Constant or Time-Dependent

Using data from Moody's corporate bond default study (1992) covering the period of 1970 to 1991, Figure 1 compares the yearly conditional default probabilities of investment grade bonds with those of BB and B rated bonds. (If conditional default probabilities were constant, those curves would be flat.) It shows that for investment grade bonds, yearly default probabilities in the future periods remain relatively constant (about 0.3%) and have a slightly increasing trend over time. On the other hand, conditional default probabilities of BB bonds peaked at year 2 and then gradually declined. B-rated bonds exhibited an even steeper conditional default profile with an astonishing 8% default rate in the first year.

FIGURE 1
Conditional Default Rates (1970-1991)

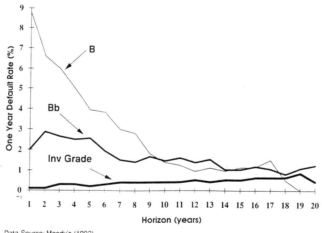

Data Source: Moody's (1992)

Note however that in using historical default rates from various studies as the basis of pricing securities, one has to examine carefully how the figures were calculated. For example, default studies by Moody's (1992) and Altman (1992a) show very similar ten-year *cumulative* default probabilities for BB and B bonds. However, if we calculate year-by-year conditional default probabilities, two studies presented different default profiles during this ten-year time period as depicted in Figure 2.

FIGURE 2
Conditional Default Rates (1970-1991)

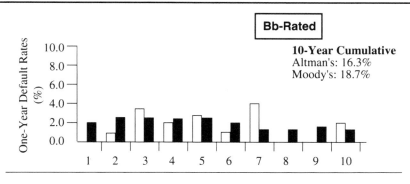

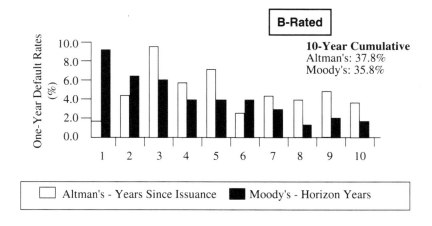

While there are a few technical differences in terms of how default rates are derived, the discrepancies of default probability curves in Figure 2 are primarily due to the fact that the two studies defined the bond universe differently. Moody's study grouped the bonds with the same ratings regardless of their ages or previous rating history. On the other hand, Altman's study tracked the bonds with the same ratings at the time of original issue. Thus, for a given bond rating, Altman's lifetime default curve is essentially the product of conditional default probabilities and bond rating change probabilities.[2] While Altman's default data reflects the expected credit profile during the *life time* of a newly issued bond, Moody's definition is more appropriate from the standpoint of pricing a *seasoned* bond.

One would assume that since default probability indicates the creditworthiness of the firm, it should apply to both private and public issues. Nevertheless, unlike public securities, private securities are normally held by a few institutional investors who often negotiate terms and provisions that address special needs of credit protection. As a result, a financially distressed condition applicable to private securities may still be a going concern condition for public issues.

In the area of commercial mortgages, the only reliable delinquency data thus far is the quarterly report published by the American Council of Life Insurance (ACLI). However, because of the lack of a large database with detailed characteristics information about mortgages and originators, there are few extensive default studies. Recent unpublished research by Snyderman (1991) examined the default experiences of more than 7,000 loans originated by seven insurance companies from 1972 to 1984. The yearly conditional default profile of commercial mortgages was similar to that of BB bonds in Figure 1 in that default rates peaked at year 2 and then decreased gradually. By disaggregating the underlying cohorts, the study also indicated that the *pattern* of default profile largely depends on economic conditions. This is similar to what has been documented in various corporate bond default studies.

Estimation of Default Probabilities

Historical default rates in the various aforementioned studies provide a good basis for pricing illiquid securities. Fons (1990) showed that micro-economic variables such as the changes in gross domestic production and in the rating mix of new issues are useful in estimating default rates. Nevertheless, historical and predicted default rates from those studies are reported only by rating category. Since neither rated nor secondary prices are available for most of illiquid securities, the following information still needs to be estimated: (1) quality ratings (or rating equivalents), (2) security specific credit risk, and (3) a default curve in the future periods. This can be achieved through the use of a quantitative credit risk evaluation model.

Credit risk modelling essentially involves extracting credit risk information embedded in the firm's various financial and accounting ratios, and in price movements of its public securities. The process has traditionally adapted one of the diverse group of statistical classification analysis. The most fundamental is discriminant analysis, which was introduced in Altman (1968) and updated to a commercially available tool (Zeta Model) in Altman et al. (1977). The model generates a continuous credit scale that weights important financial variables according to their contributions to the overall credit risk. Recent discussion has focused the advantages of alternative techniques, such as logistic regression (Martin (1977)) and recursive partitioning analysis (Frydman et al. (1985)).[3] The latter produces a conventional decision tree with terminal nodes representing different discrete risk categories.

A credit score or risk category from these models represents an estimate of the likelihood of failure of the firm that is intended only for a single investment horizon, for example, one year. For pricing securities, a series of failure probabilities extending over the life of the particular instrument is required. To derive such a default time curve, one needs to use historical default curves by credit rating (such as Moody's or Altman's) in conjunction with credit scores or risk categories.

A more direct way to estimate default time profile is to use a survival analysis approach. This approach originated in the biostatistics literature when medical researchers were concerned with how a particular treatment would affect a patient's survival probability over an extended period.[4] The method is rather new in credit research and has not been adopted for commercial use. While the basic analysis assumes a particular form of the survival curve, recent research by Wilson and Kallberg (1990) has used the partial logistic approach developed by Efron (1988) to allow more general specifications. This reference also shows (empirically and theoretically) that rank ordering of firm's creditworthiness can change over time. That is, firm A can be less risky than firm B over a one-year investment horizon, but significantly more risky over a five-year horizon.

Applying Credit Risk Models

The theory and methodologies of building a corporate credit risk model are simple but actual implementation is found to be difficult, especially for lower credit quality companies. Kallberg and Kao (1988) provides a checklist of issues to be considered in the credit risk modelling process. When applying a credit risk model to evaluating private securities, one also has to recognize that some critical financial variables found to be significant in numerous credit risk models may not be directly available from private securities (e.g., ratio of market value of equities to total capitalization).

Moreover, in using financial accounting information as the input to a credit model, credit risk evaluation is assumed to update only on a quarterly basis with approximately a month delay of reporting. As a result, from a pricing viewpoint, the value between two financial reporting dates is essentially affected only by the changes in the discount functions (and their volatilities), not by the changes in the adjustment factors (A_i) in the equation on page 52. Toward this end, one alternative is to derive default probabilities embedded in the price movements of all the *publicly traded* securities of a firm and their corresponding priorities in the firm's capital structure.[5] While this method can provide more timely estimates, it suffers the same drawbacks that existing pricing approaches have as mentioned in the section above, *Existing Pricing Approaches*. Additionally, it stringently assumes that the public security investors provide unbiased and timely assessment of the firm's credit risk.

Commercial Mortgage Default Estimation

With mortgages, almost all of current research focuses on estimating default risk of residential mortgages. One notable study of commercial mortgage default estimation is the model proposed by Vandell (1990) that is based on the equity theory of mortgage default (i.e., the likelihood of default given the relative market values of the loan balance to collateral.) The model relates commercial mortgage foreclosure rates to loan term, lending rates and commitments in the mortgage market, and the property's market value.

In view of the recent issue of commercial mortgage-backed securities by Resolution Trust Corporation, rating agencies are designing rating criteria which are important for evaluating the delinquency risk of commercial mortgages. In addition, an ambitious research project is being initiated by the Society of Actuaries and the American Council of Life Insurance to examine credit risk events and associated economic losses in private placements and commercial mortgages (see Barry and Luckner (1992)). Hopefully, their efforts and future availability of more comprehensive databases will result in more extensive research and better understanding of the credit risk of commercial mortgages and private placements.

RECOVERY RATES

Private Debt

The salvage value in the equation above is essentially the present value of cash flows received by defaulted securities at the time of either reorganization or liquidation from a bankruptcy (or default) process. The difficulty in calculating the present value of loss recovery stems from the fact that (1) the forms of actual payments at settlement (e.g., equity swaps, debt exchanges or asset sales) are normally complex to value, (2) the time required to resolve the bankruptcy process (becoming liquidated or reorganized) varies,[6] and (3) the detailed information about securities or the firm at default or settlement are difficult to obtain. As a result, most studies of recovery rates simply used *trading prices* of the defaulted securities as a proxy.

Altman (1992a) indicated that the average recovery prices on defaulted debt decline as priority in capital structure is lowered. They ranged from an averaged $60.5 per $100 face amount for secured bonds to almost $28 for subordinated debt in the period of 1985 to 1991. Altman's results are similar to those from the Moody's survey which covered a longer period of 1974 to 1991. However, both studies showed widely different recovery prices from one year to another. For deferred interest subordinated debt, Altman's study also indicated that their recovery prices on average were $2.5 lower than those of cash-pay debt in 1990 and 1991.

Another possible source for expected recovery rates is the assumptions used by rating agencies in rating CBOs (Collateralized Bond Obligations). Moody's assumes a 30% loss recovery on all defaulted collateral including accrued interest but does not allow any cash flow delay upon default. On the other hand, Standard and Poor's assumes a 40%, 25% and 15% recovery for senior secured, senior and subordinated collateral, respectively. However, it does not include accrued interest but allows 6 months of cash flow delays.

Commercial Mortgages

According to ACLI's quarterly survey (1992), delinquency rates of commercial mortgages have increased from 2.7% in December 1986 to 6.4% in first quarter of 1992. When a mortgage is delinquent, it may be in one of the two states: in-foreclosure or not in-foreclosure. The percentage of in-foreclosures has increased from 32% of delinquent mortgages in 1986 to 50% in first quarter of 1992. Snyderman (1991) reported that an in-foreclosure mortgage historically took about three years to recover 68% of its principal plus the interest accrued since the beginning of delinquency. On the other hand, a delinquent mortgage that was not in-foreclosure took about one year to recover the principal and accrued interest. The recovery rate on such mortgages is expected to be higher than in-foreclosure mortgages.

PERFORMANCE MEASUREMENT

Participants of illiquid securities markets have no universally recognized performance benchmarks due to lack of pricing and comprehensive data-bases. In the area of private placements, one can develop a benchmark from various bond and/or equity indices designed for publicly traded markets (e.g., equal weights of A, BBB and BB-rated corporate bond indices). However, the user should be aware of the fundamental structure differences between private and public securities markets. Moreover, such a customized benchmark needs to be adjusted for several unique features of illiquid security investments.

First of all, an illiquidity premium may be added. The magnitude of this return component is highly debatable and difficult to estimate. Often, nominal yield differentials between private placements and publicly-traded bonds cannot provide an accurate indicator because of their vast differences in terms, covenants and option-like features. However, an illiquidity premium should be consistent with the investor's expectation of value-added of participating in illiquid markets vis-à-vis publicly traded markets.

If one combines various public bond market indices to derive a customized benchmark, the relative public market values of those performance components may not be relevant to the investors. The weights should reflect the investor's expectation regarding the long term allocation of each market segment in his overall private placement portfolios or private debt markets in general.

In addition, illiquidity of those securities dictates that the change in the portfolio asset mix can only be accomplished very gradually. Thus, to select initial "long term normal" sector weights, one should allow an adjustment period during which the relative weight of each sector changes gradually toward "long-term norm." Otherwise, in evaluating performance attributes, the deviation from long term asset mix will become a portfolio manager's active bet even though it only reflects the investor's inability to shift the sector mix freely.

Finally, almost all the public bond indices assume that cash flow is reinvested in the same index. Practically, this is almost impossible for illiquid asset investors who often sweep any cash distributions to a cash account. A meaningful illiquid asset benchmark should reflect such a practice.

Commercial Mortgage Performance Benchmark

Although there is no publicly available benchmark for commercial mortgage investments, survey information about mortgage origination, rates and delinquencies can serve as a basis for constructing a meaningful benchmark.[7] Corcoran (1989) presented a return series of commercial mortgage versus corporate bonds. The return series contains one single mortgage and does not take into account the loss from delinquency. Snyderman (1990) also proposed a default-free commercial mortgage index that assumes an unrealistic mortgage investment process of buying a new mortgage and holding it for a month. Giliberto (1990) employed a simple delinquency loss assumption in his *quarterly* commercial mortgage return series. However, the index construction and return calculations were based *only* on ACLI survey information that has significant time lag.[8] None of the above return series is updated and available to the public. General Motors Investment Management Corporation (GMIMCo) tracks a proprietary monthly commercial mortgage index that fully utilizes the timely mortgage survey information and quantitative techniques for fixed-income valuation. This index, including new and seasoned mortgages, has features (described below) that make it investable and replicable.

Since there is no information about every "outstanding" commercial mortgage in the market, the construction of this index involves purchasing a new, hypothetical mortgage at the beginning of each month starting at the time that the first commercial mortgage investment commences. As a passive strategy, the maturity and contract rate of each new "average" mortgage is defined by the survey data and the mortgage is assumed to be amortized from day one following a thirty-year schedule. In order to reduce the turnover and transaction costs, each mortgage is held in the index to its maturity or to an expected holding period (stated in the long-term investment policy), whichever comes first. When a mortgage is deleted from the index, it is replaced by a then newly originated "average" mortgage. At the end of each month, each seasoned mortgage in the index is repriced off a newly originated mortgage with comparable maturity. Cash flow (interest income and principal paydowns) is treated as a cash distribution. The index is price-weighted.

Unlike any public bond index where a bond may be deleted from the index due to upgrade, downgrade or default, the mortgages in this index remain default free if we follow the construction process above. Thus, to be consistent with other bond market indices and to make this index replicable, it is necessary to incorporate the default probability and default loss in the index calculation. The delinquency process and survey information described in the section on Commercial Mortgages above, can be used to calculate the potential loss and recovery.

First, given the proportions of in-foreclosure and not-in-foreclosure, the *expected* cash flow (principal and accrued interests) from the delinquency date to the recovery date can be calculated. Then, the difference between the *scheduled* monthly income return and the internal rate of return from future cash streams of a delinquent mortgage represents the loss in basis point from delinquency.

The delinquency loss has increased every year since 1987 resulting in a rate of 58 basis points per year. As of the first quarter of 1992, the loss from mortgage delinquency was running about 8 basis points per month or 97 basis points per year. It should be noted that due to a lack of detailed delinquency information, the above calculation makes the following three assumptions: (1) delinquency rates are the same for new and seasoned mortgages although historically it has not been the case; (2) it does not take into account the loss from the modification of terms and conditions of the original mortgages; and (3) historical recovery rates for delinquent mortgages are used in the calculation. One should expect that recovery rates of delinquent mortgages would be lower in the bear market. However, the impact of the recovery rate assumption on the delinquency loss calculation is considerably lower than the delinquency rate itself.

RETURN CALCULATION

The standards of computing and measuring performance have been addressed by various entities over the past twenty-five years: Bank Administration Institute in 1968, Trust Universe Comparison Service (TUCS) in 1980 and Association for Investment Management Research (AIMR) in 1989. Computational methodologies are often considered basic and the importance of different return measures are well understood. However, actual performance reporting in the investment community neglects some of the basic principles of performance measurement.

For example, it is well known that the dollar-weighted return provides a measure of the *economic* performance of assets and the time-weighted return indicates the performance of a *constant* dollar in the asset. Removing the impact of different cash flow patterns, the time-weighted return is used to compare the performance with other managers or other assets. Also, the time-weighted return is often the only performance figure reported.

However, in the situation where the timing of contributions and withdrawals *can* be controlled by a portfolio manager, the dollar-weighted return is an important and reliable performance figure. It shows exactly how each dollar was utilized over time and is affected by the timing and size of contributions to and disbursements from the assets. This situation is particularly important to a portfolio manager investing in illiquid securities since (1) capital draw-downs and distributions are normally made by asset managers; (2) security purchase and liquidation are achieved gradually over time; and (3) cash inflow and outflow are often extraordinarily large vis-à-vis the value of the existing asset.

It is important for an illiquid asset investor to include the dollar-weighted return as supplemental performance information in addition to the time-weighted return. To show the difference between the dollar-weighted and time-weighted returns, a simulation is conducted as follows: from 12/31/1986 to 12/31/1991, $5 million was invested in the First Boston High Yield Bond Index at the beginning of each quarter for a total cost of $100 million. (This cash flow scenario is *not uncommon* for private market investments.) Given this capital infusion pattern, the dollar-weighted return over the five-year period was 11.86% per year. The time-weighted return of this portfolio was 152 basis points lower—10.34% per year.

Finally, the calculation of the exact time-weighted return involves the valuation of assets prior to the occurrence of cash flows. This requirement makes the time-weighted return calculation of illiquid assets or the assets with many large cash flows extremely difficult or time consuming. Consequently, almost all the performance reports adopt an approximation method that essentially smooths the impact of intra-period cash flow by adjusting the asset values only at the beginning and ending of the period. Depending on the size of cash flow and the volatility of asset values, the difference between the "exact" and "approximate" returns can be as significant as that between the dollar and time-weighted returns.

CONCLUSION

Traditionally, pricing an illiquid security involves assuming yields or yield spreads that are highly subjective. Together with the lack of publicly recognized benchmarks, risk and return of illiquid security investments are often misunderstood. The increasing interest in these securities by various institutional investors and regulatory agencies shows a need for a more objective pricing framework.

While using pricing information from publicly traded fixed-income markets presents a viable alternative, it does not address the fundamental issues of pricing illiquid assets. The main problem is the estimation of the changes in the security's credit quality rating and the firm's specific credit risk. This article reviews a default risk based pricing approach that incorporates recent research in the areas of default rate, credit risk and capital structure. More importantly, the model can be easily blended into recent developed term structure theories and option pricing models.

Publicly traded fixed-income indices can be used as a basis for illiquid asset performance benchmarks. Adjustments have to be made to reflect the unique nature of illiquid asset investments. A proprietary commercial mortgage index is presented here. The features of this index are consistent with general principles of popular public bond index construction and fixed-income security valuation. The index is considered investable and replicable. Lastly, those investing in illiquid assets should be aware of the ambiguities in the calculation and the use of various return measures, particularly of the interpretation of discrepancy between the dollar and time-weighted returns.

NOTES

1. There are numerous empirical studies on illiquidity premia in equity markets. For a summary discussion, see Pratt (1990).
2. In fact, we can compare the first year conditional default prob abilities in Altman's and Moody's studies since all the bonds have the same ratings. The default rate differentials (2% and 6% for BB and B bonds, respectively) indicate that (1) the age of the bond affects default likelihood and/or (2) future default probability is correlated with past default history.
3. Recursive partitioning analysis is a powerful nonparametric technique, particularly useful for relatively small data sets.
4. A number of good references to survival analysis exist; see Cox and Oakes (1984).
5. For example, Queen and Roll (1987) applied security market data such as price, total return, return volatility and security beta to predict a firm's survival probabilities. It should be noted that this study examined the firm's mortality from the viewpoint of its equity trading status.
6. Altman (1992b) studied the reorganization experiences of 284 firms under Chapter 11. During the period of 1979 to 1991, about 54% of the sample cases received plan confirmation within one and one-half years after the petition date while 13% took more than three years. The average time of reorganization was 21 months (with a median of 17 months). Successful reorganization generally takes a longer time than liquidation.
7. Some investors use the return of publicly traded BBB corporate bond index plus a premium as the benchmark performance. This practice has low correlation with that in commercial mortgage spreads. Allowing for a time lag relationship, the correlation improves only marginally.
8. Currently the survey information is reported with a time lag of at least three months. Since April 1989, ACLI has reported only *quarterly average* figures.

REFERENCES

Altman, Edward I., 1968, Financial ratios, discriminant analysis and the prediction of corporate bankruptcy, *The Journal of Finance* 23, 589-609.

Altman, Edward I., 1992a, Defaults and returns on high yield bonds, *Merrill Lynch High Yield Securities Research.*

Altman, Edward I., 1992b, Evaluating the Chapter 11 bankruptcy reorganization process, *New York University Salomon Center Working Paper Series* S-92-22.

Altman, Edward I., Robert, G. Haldeman and R. Narayanan, 1977, Zeta analysis: a new model to identify bankruptcy risk of corporations, *Journal of Banking and Finance* 1, 29-54.

American Council of Life Insurance, 1992, Quarterly survey of mortgage loan delinquencies and foreclosures, *Investment Bulletin.*

Barry, Gery, J. and Warren R. Luckner, 1992, Study of economic loss associated with credit risk, *The Actuary*, 9-12.

Bierman, Harold Jr. and Jerome E. Hass, 1975, An analytic model of bond risk differentials, *Journal of Financial and Quantitative Analysis* 10, 757-773.

Blackwell, David, W. and David S. Kidwell, 1988, An investigation of cost differences between public and private placements of debt, *Journal of Financial Economics* 22, 253-278.

Corcoran, Patrick J., 1989, Commercial mortgages: measuring risk and return, *The Journal of Portfolio Management* Winter, 69-73.

Cox, D. R. and D. Oakes, 1984, *Analysis of Survival Data* (Chapman and Hall, New York, NY).

Efron, B., 1988, Logistic regression, survival analysis and the Kaplan–Meier curve, *Journal of the American Statistical Association* 83, 414-425.

Fisher, Lawrence, 1959, Determinants of risk premiums on corporate bonds, *The Journal of Political Economy*, 217-237.

Fons, Jerome S., 1992, An approach to forecasting default rates, *Moody's Special Report.*

Frydman, Halina, Edward I. Altman and Duen-Li Kao, 1985, Introducing recursive partitioning for financial classification: the case of financial distress, *The Journal of Finance* 40, 269-291.

Giliberto, Michael S., 1991, Commercial mortgages as a pension fund alternative, *Salomon Brothers Bond Market Research–Real Estate.*

Hempel, George H. and Donald G. Simonson, 1992, The case for comprehensive market-value reporting, *Bank Accounting and Finance* 5, 23-29.

Ho, Thomas Y. S., 1990, *Strategic Fixed-Income Investment* (Dow Jones–Irwin, Homewood, IL).

Kallberg, Jarl G. and Duen-Li Kao, 1988, Statistical models in credit management, in Y. Kim, ed.: *Advances in Working Capital Management* (JAI Press, Greenwich, CT), 147-174.

Martin, D., 1977, Early warning of bank failure: a logit regression approach, *Journal of Banking and Finance* 1, 259-276.

Moody's Special Report, 1992, Corporate bond defaults and default rates: 1970-1991.

Morris, David M., 1992, The case against market–value accounting: a pragmatic view, *Bank Accounting and Finance* 5, 30-36.

Pratt, Shannon P., 1990, Discounts and premia, in E. Theodore Veit, ed.: *Valuation of Closely Held Companies and Inactively Traded Securities* (The Institute of Chartered Financial Analysts, Charlottesville, VA), 38-50.

Queen, Maggie and Richard Roll, 1987, Firm mortality: using market indicators to predict survival, *Financial Analysts Journal,* May-June.

Rodriguez, Richardo J., 1988, Default risk, yield spreads, and time to maturity, *Journal of Financial and Quantitative Analysis* 23, 111-117.

Silvers, J. B., 1973, An alternative to the yield spread as a measure of risk, *The Journal of Finance*, 933-955.

Snyderman, Mark P., 1990, A commercial mortgage performance index, *The Journal of Portfolio Management* Spring, 70-73.

Snyderman, Mark P., 1991, Commercial mortgages: default occurrence and estimated yield impact, *The Journal of Portfolio Management* Fall, 82-87.

Vandell, Kerry, 1990, Predicting commercial mortgage foreclosure experience, *Salomon Brothers Bond Market Research*.

Wilson, Barry K. and Jarl G. Kallberg, 1990, A partial logistic approach to firm failure analysis, *New York University Working Paper Series*.

Yawitz, Jess B., Kevin J. Maloney and Louis H. Ederington, 1985, *The Journal of Finance* 40, 1127-1140.

Yawitz, Jess B., 1977, An analytical model of interest rate differentials and different default recoveries, *Journal of Financial and Quantitative Analysis* 12, 481-491.

Zwick, Burton, 1980, Yields on privately placed corporate bonds, *The Journal of Finance* 35, 23-29.

CHAPTER 5

ENHANCING THE RETURNS OF A REPLICATING PORTFOLIO

William F. McCoy, CFA
Financial Strategies Consultant, Global Advanced Technology Corporation

INTRODUCTION

There has been remarkable growth in passive portfolio management over the last decade. For fixed-income portfolios, index management is more difficult because it is not possible to purchase all of the bonds in the benchmark. For insurance companies or pension plan sponsors, the benchmark does not contain bonds at all. The problem is usually solved by deciding on various measures of risk and creating a replicating portfolio with those characteristics. If it is possible to define and match risk characteristics, then it is also possible to "tilt" the replicating portfolio toward various risk characteristics to outperform the index, when appropriate.

The ability to create portfolios with targeted risk and return characteristics, focuses the investment decision process on the appropriate rules for portfolio construction and trading. In an article entitled, "Using Key Rate Duration to Replicate a Treasury Index," McCoy (1991) demonstrates that key rate duration is a superior way of controlling for interest-rate risk, while holding other sources of risk constant. This chapter describes the results of holding the key rate durations of an index constant – thereby controlling for interest-rate risk – and examines the possibility of outperforming that index by constructing portfolios tilted toward cheap/rich,

William F. McCoy is Financial Strategies Consultant, Global Advanced Technology Corporation, 40 Wall Street, New York, New York, 10005.

convexity, coupon, or portfolio turnover. The additional return generated by the various strategies ranges from 22 basis points to 238 basis points. Turnover, an important part of any set of trading rules, can be managed by this process.

REPLICATING A TREASURY INDEX

There are many ways of replicating a Treasury index. One method is to choose various characteristics of the index and then to create a matrix of those measures. Each cell of the matrix is then filled with bonds that match the average characteristics of that cell. However, the main drawbacks of this method are how the characteristics are chosen. First, the characteristics are often attributes of the index, and not truly sources of risk or return. For instance, coupon and maturity are attributes that are often targeted. However, duration is a better measurement of the risk. Second, the number of cells used is arbitrary.

Another method is to target the appropriate risk characteristics and create a portfolio to match those. The commonly accepted characteristics are duration, convexity, price and yield. However, duration is only a measure of parallel interest-rate risk. Should the spot curve move in a nonparallel fashion, the replicating portfolio would have different returns than the index.

Key Rate Duration is a measure of the nonparallel interest-rate risk of a portfolio. Just as effective duration is based on a parallel shift of the curve, each key rate duration is based on a shift of a segment of the curve. Thus, the key rate duration of a security or portfolio is a vector of numbers, representing the interest sensitivity to various areas of the yield curve. If all of the segments of the curve shift simultaneously, then a parallel shift occurs, and the key rate durations sum to the effective duration. Therefore, key rate duration is a more complete concept than effective duration.

McCoy (1991) demonstrates the effectiveness of using key rate durations to match the returns of a Treasury Index. The study was performed from January 1990 to December 1990. Both one-month and three-month horizons were studied. Three methods of controlling interest-rate risk were used. The first was an effective duration match. The second was based on four key rate durations; the third on 11 key rate durations.

Over the year studied, the average absolute difference in returns was calculated in basis points. That is, the portfolio was penalized as much for being over as for being under the index. The results were as follows:

FIGURE 1
Matching (errors in basis points)

	Eff Dur	4 Key Rate Dur	11 Key Rate Dur
1 month	8	3	2
3 month	12	8	5

The results are even more dramatic when the single worst error is considered. For the one-month horizon, the effective duration match had a maximum error of 30 basis points, the four key rate duration match had a maximum error of 7 basis points, and the 11 key rate duration match had a maximum error of 4 basis points. The ability of key rate durations to control interest-rate risk was thus clearly demonstrated.

In addition to controlling for interest-rate risk, other characteristics of the portfolio were controlled. These were convexity, average price, average rich/cheap, yield to worst and percent of callable securities. These characteristics were constrained to control for other sources of return. Moreover, the portfolio had a "null" objective function. That is, any set of bonds that met the characteristics were acceptable. The current study biased the portfolio toward some of the portfolio characteristics.

ENHANCED TREASURY INDEX STUDY

The current study constructed portfolios on the last business day from December 1989 to December 1991. The portfolios were held for one month, the returns generated, and the turnover examined from the previous portfolio. GAT's Treasury Index was used as the universe for the optimization and the basis for comparison. All portfolios matched the key rate duration profile of the Treasury index, while other characteristics of the portfolio were varied. No transaction costs were assumed.

The first set of portfolios extended the performance of the 11 key rate duration match. As shown in Figure 1 Column A, the average absolute error increased from 2 basis points to 3 basis points. The median absolute error, which was not reported previously, is 2 basis points. The maximum error increased from 4 basis points to 12 basis points. Clearly, key rate duration is a robust method to match a Treasury index over time.

FIGURE 2

	Treasury Index 1 Month	(A) KRD1-11 1 Month	(B) Min Turn 1 Month	(C) Cheap 1 Month	(D) Rich 1 Month	(E) Max Cnx 1 Month	(F) Min Cpn 1 Month
Dec-89	-1.42	-1.39	-1.39	-1.38	-1.50	-1.42	-1.46
Jan-90	0.07	0.10	0.05	0.19	-0.21	0.08	0.06
Feb-90	0.04	0.04	0.04	0.11	0.01	0.09	0.03
Mar-90	-0.93	-0.95	-0.97	-0.88	-0.99	-0.91	-0.91
Apr-90	2.76	2.78	2.72	2.79	2.67	2.77	2.75
May-90	1.58	1.58	1.62	1.63	1.51	1.60	1.56
Jun-90	1.28	1.27	1.39	1.33	1.23	1.27	1.33
Jul-90	-1.49	-1.45	-1.34	-1.40	-1.53	-1.49	-1.45
Aug-90	0.98	1.01	0.97	1.04	0.95	0.98	0.98
Sep-90	1.65	1.64	1.71	1.68	1.59	1.63	1.66
Oct-90	2.20	2.20	2.28	2.25	2.17	2.21	2.27
Nov-90	1.61	1.59	1.77	1.66	1.59	1.63	1.62
Dec-90	1.04	1.05	1.20	1.11	0.94	1.10	1.08
Jan-91	0.55	0.55	0.69	0.57	0.48	0.56	0.57
Feb-91	0.45	0.44	0.49	0.49	0.43	0.48	0.42
Mar-91	1.10	1.07	1.05	1.16	0.98	1.11	1.07
Apr-91	0.40	0.38	0.49	0.45	0.34	0.42	0.40
May-91	-0.61	-0.16	-0.19	-0.13	-0.19	-0.15	-0.18
Jun-91	1.23	1.21	1.19	1.31	1.07	1.26	1.17
Jul-91	2.33	2.37	2.45	2.42	2.32	2.43	2.41
Aug-91	2.08	2.15	2.21	2.23	2.05	2.16	2.15
Sep-91	0.87	0.95	0.99	1.34	0.74	0.86	0.86
Oct-91	1.00	0.99	1.07	1.23	0.98	0.99	0.97
Nov-91	3.43	3.55	3.55	3.61	3.41	3.51	3.55
Dec-91	-1.63	-1.54	-1.53	-1.49	-1.68	-1.58	-1.70
Avg Abs Error		3	8				
Median Abs Error		2	7				
Maximum Abs Error		12	16				
Cumulative Return	23.04%	23.54%	24.86%	25.87%	21.02%	23.73%	23.26%
Cumulative Outperformance	0.50%	1.83%		2.83%	-2.01%	0.69%	0.22%
Average Monthly Outperformance (bp)				9	-7	2	1
Median Monthly Outperformance (bp)				6	-5	1	0
Greatest Outperformance (bp)				47	-1	10	12
Worst Outperformance (bp)				2	-28	-2	-7

The next set of portfolios matched the key rate durations, but tilted the portfolio toward certain sources of returns. First, cheap and rich portfolios were constructed. Based on GAT's spot curve methodology, it is possible to attribute a theoretical price to a security. From the theoretical and observed prices, the security can be deemed rich or cheap. If a portfolio is constructed of cheap securities, it should outperform the index. If a portfolio is constructed of rich securities, it should underperform the index.

As Figure 1 Columns C and D demonstrate, the cheap portfolio had a cumulative outperformance of 283 basis points. The rich portfolio had a cumulative underperformance of -201 basis points. On average, the cheap portfolio added 6 to 9 basis points of outperformance a month, while the rich portfolio subtracted 5 to 7 basis points. Never did the cheap portfolio underperform the portfolio, and never did the rich portfolio outperform the index.

Obviously, the bad price of a single security could skew these results. However, Treasury prices tend to be better reported. Secondly, during the spot curve estimation, the average error in pricing the bonds to the spot curve is computed. The correlation between the average error at the time the portfolio is constructed to its outperformance is .36. As the level of the correlation suggests, the outperformance is not due to the mispricing of a single security, but several securities.

The next portfolio examined was the most convex portfolio possible. Positive convexity always adds to security returns, as long as interest rates fluctuate. However, should interest rates remain stable, convexity adds nothing to a portfolio. Figure 1 Column E shows the results of holding the maximum convex portfolio. Over the time studied, it had a cumulative outperformance of 69 basis points. That translates to 1 basis point to 2 basis points per month, on average. The worst it ever did over this period was to underperform the index by 2 basis points. Confirming that the return due to convexity is related to volatility, the correlation between the outperformance and one-year spot volatility is .35.

The final portfolio examined minimized the average coupon of the portfolio. Over time with a positively sloped yield curve, the reinvestment of coupon cash flows should lower the realized yield of the bond. However, for a zero coupon bond, if rates do not fluctuate, the "coupon" is accreted toward par. The realized return is closer to that of the yield than with a coupon bond. However, if the markets are efficient, then this phenomenon should be recognized and not possible. Figure 1 Column F shows the results of holding the minimum coupon portfolio. Clearly, this was the weakest of the portfolios studied. Over the entire time period, minimizing coupon added 22 basis points of outperformance to the portfolio, which averages to 0 to 1 basis point per month. At its best, the strategy added 12 basis points; at its worst, it subtracted 17 basis points. While this strategy might work better over a longer time frame, it does not appear to have much potential.

FIGURE 3

	(A) KRD1-11 1 Month	(B) Turnover 1 Month	(C) Cheap 1 Month	(D) Rich 1 Month	(E) Max Cnx 1 Month	(F) Min Cpn 1 Month
Dec-89						
Jan-90	83.11	46.93	74.04	73.09	52.61	71.05
Feb-90	84.36	30.33	79.87	68.11	86.73	62.19
Mar-90	71.24	49.60	67.96	54.61	82.25	66.03
Apr-90	90.30	44.69	75.94	64.69	53.61	59.56
May-90	79.01	33.16	73.35	85.77	89.14	48.21
Jun-90	75.23	34.57	80.29	67.81	80.21	58.91
Jul-90	82.97	30.25	82.92	58.04	87.62	64.73
Aug-90	82.92	38.32	85.72	73.73	67.61	55.88
Sep-90	72.41	21.93	82.38	81.78	84.58	84.81
Oct-90	83.10	35.85	58.98	58.62	77.57	63.92
Nov-90	87.19	43.35	62.50	68.76	69.81	51.59
Dec-90	71.47	25.98	71.57	62.71	80.48	70.84
Jan-91	90.40	10.88	53.55	72.58	77.60	58.30
Feb-91	88.79	13.39	79.17	64.44	78.04	41.54
Mar-91	77.65	29.75	92.36	50.61	89.74	73.90
Apr-91	80.85	24.51	74.72	85.28	84.99	73.23
May-91	73.10	19.67	77.15	62.39	85.15	63.37
Jun-91	67.63	42.14	79.28	58.66	82.57	65.07
Jul-91	91.56	34.81	58.27	71.60	80.46	75.97
Aug-91	80.69	43.47	77.23	73.03	86.84	32.24
Sep-91	66.27	35.90	92.05	77.26	69.30	68.08
Oct-91	72.63	29.92	77.85	74.10	73.70	69.95
Nov-91	85.02	35.49	98.24	64.82	94.79	78.42
Dec-91	61.37	36.71	84.79	76.73	76.33	69.08
Average Monthly Turnover						
	79.13	32.98	76.67	68.72	78.82	63.62
Median Monthly Turnover						
	80.77	34.69	77.54	68.43	80.47	64.90

Turnover is an important part of all portfolio strategies. The additional returns earned through exploiting opportunities can be lost in transaction costs. Figure 2 demonstrates the outperformance of various strategies versus the Treasury Index; Columns A, C-F shows the turnover of the portfolios over time. The average and median turnover is fairly high and consistent across portfolios. The only exception is minimizing coupon, with a turnover 10% less than the others. However, this does not demonstrate that the strategies discussed are unworkable. The portfolios were constructed from scratch each time. No attempt was made to control for turnover. In addition, the level of turnover to outperform the index is actually slightly less than to replicate it. Thus, if a portfolio is being constructed or rebalanced, for a similar level of turnover, additional return can be earned.

Up to now, turnover has been treated as a result of portfolio activity. However, it is possible manage the level of turnover in a portfolio. Another portfolio was constructed that had the same constraint set as the replicating portfolio, except it minimized turnover from the previously held portfolio. As shown in Figure 2 Column B, this portfolio has turnover level 1/2 to 2/3 less than the replicating portfolio. Moreover, as shown in Figure 1 Column B, the average absolute error versus the replicating portfolio went from 3 basis points to 8 basis points. The turnover could have been less, if the constraint set had been relaxed. Thus, turnover can be controlled in a portfolio.

FIGURE 4
Monthly Return Difference vs Treasury Index

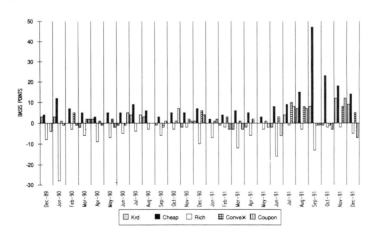

CONCLUSION

Key Rate Duration continues to serve as an effective means of controlling the interest-rate risk of a portfolio. Moreover, coupled with highly convex portfolios biased toward cheap securities, while avoiding rich securities, it appears possible to add value to an index. While the turnover of the portfolios appears high, turnover can be controlled. Moreover, in any ongoing portfolio strategy, turnover is an attribute that should be controlled. A future study will examine the possibilities of controlling and monitoring portfolio performance and turnover.

CHAPTER 6

MANAGING FIXED-INCOME ASSETS WITHIN A MULTI-ASSET CLASS INSURANCE PORTFOLIO

Robert M. Lally

Director of Portfolio Strategies, Metropolitan Life

INTRODUCTION

In his landmark essay, F.M. Reddington (1952) defined immunization as "the investment of assets in such a way that the existing business is immune to a general change in the rate of interest." Reddington and other early "immunization pioneers" identified the following necessary conditions for this earliest form of immunization:

a. The present value of assets must equal the present value of liabilities.

b. The convexity of the assets must exceed the convexity of the liabilities.

c. The yield curve must be completely flat.

d. The yield curve shifts must be instantaneous, small and parallel.

e. Embedded options free fixed-income instruments can only be used to back the liability.

Robert M. Lally is Director of Portfolio Strategies, Metropolitan Life, One Madison Avenue, New York, New York, 10010.

While Reddington's work represents a very valuable contribution, it serves as a point of departure for many portfolio managers responsible for assets tied to a liability. For these managers, the pristine conditions required by Reddington are not their reality. Specifically,

a. The PV of their assets will most likely not equal the PV of their liability.

b. Adding convexity to portfolios backing liabilities with significant "tails" [1] may be too expensive or the implementation of a barbell strategy may subject the portfolio to an inordinate amount of yield curve twist risk (i.e., convexity's "dark side") as to be rendered undesirable. Moreover, they may decide (or may have to do so for spread purposes) to purchase negatively convex fixed-income securities with embedded options.

c. They are most likely operating in a sloped yield curve environment.

d. Their portfolios are subjected to numerous forms of large and small nonparallel yield curve shifts.

e. In addition to holding bonds with embedded options, their portfolios may contain non-fixed-income assets (e.g., equities) with limited, if any, "immunization value." [2]

As portfolio managers in the insurance industry, my colleagues and I must address this question: How do investment professionals take immunization out of the theoretical context and make it work under these real world conditions?

Although the title of this chapter is "Managing Fixed-Income Assets within a Multi-Asset Class Insurance Portfolio," it could just as appropriately have been entitled "The Custom Bond Index: A Tool for Asset Allocation, Performance Measurement and Portfolio Management." This chapter presents an analytical approach for managing fixed-income assets backing insurance, or other liabilities, where the custom bond index (CBI) is the investment professional's key decision making tool throughout the investment process.

HOW MUCH EQUITY VS. FIXED INCOME?

When investment professionals discuss asset allocation strategies, they often debate a philosophical issue with respect to equities. I have reduced the debate for equities to a **Want to Have** argument, a **Nice to Have** argument and a **Need to Have** argument.

The **Want to Have** argument is based upon the spectacular results of the equity market since the mid-1970s. The asset allocation strategies of plan sponsors are largely predicated upon this argument and result in equity allocations in excess of 50%.

FIGURE 1
"Want to Have" Rationale

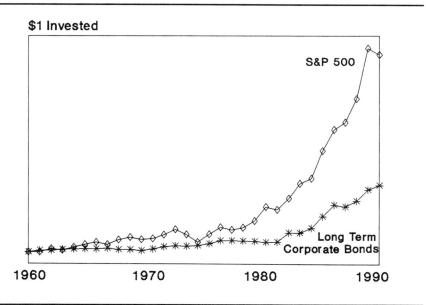

$1 Invested

As the above graph for 1990 indicates, this approach is not without its hazards. Equity returns were down by 3% while fixed-income and, presumably, liability returns were up 6% for a 9% differential. Thus, one must be comfortable with the fact that equity returns may move in the *opposite* direction of liability returns before embracing this approach. Professionals who elect to use this approach typically apply mean variance analysis for making their allocation decisions but, unfortunately, their results are extremely sensitive to their capital markets assumptions (Yoon (1992)).

The **Nice to Have** argument is based upon a convenient rule such as designating all liability cash flows beyond year thirty (or what is commonly referred to as the "tail") to be backed by equities. This argument states that tail cash flows should be backed by equities because there are very few fixed-income securities with maturities beyond thirty years to cover these liabilities.

FIGURE 2
"Nice to Have" Rationale

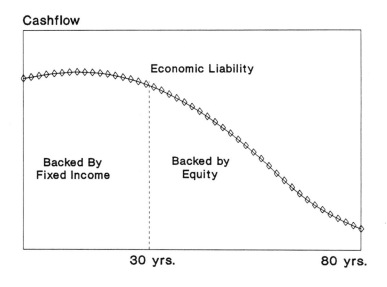

Other common convenient rules are based upon the investment horizon employed to best utilize equities' historical return advantage over fixed-income securities. For example, all liability cash flows beyond 10 years would be backed by equities if the investment time horizon for asset allocation purposes had been defined as ten years. In another approach, all cash flows beyond the duration of the long bond, which also approximates ten years, would be backed by equities.

The **Need to Have** argument is based upon using equities as a last resort. The question the **Need to Have** approach attempts to answer is: "What is the *minimum* amount of equities required to satisfy the economic liability?" The economic liability can be defined as the amount that must be paid to an insurance company's customers as well as an allowance for expenses and profits.

FIGURE 3
"Need to Have" Rational

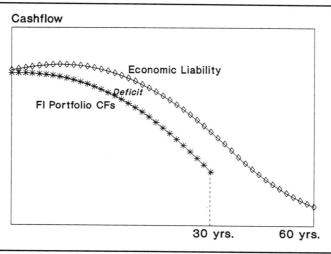

Cashflow

Economic Liability

Deficit

FI Portfolio CFs

30 yrs.   60 yrs.

For insurance companies, I advocate the **Need to Have** approach for the following reasons:

- *Insurance companies cannot "go back to the well."*
  Most insurance contracts effectively do not obligate the contractholder to pay a carrier incremental premiums for negative experience, including negative experience resulting from the underperformance of equities. In contrast, a defined benefit pension plan can obtain incremental contributions from the sponsor for negative experience. This helps to explains why insurance companies have lower perceived risk tolerance than pension plans.

- *Insurance products are priced by actuaries based upon fixed-income market-derived yield and spot rate information.*
  Actuaries generally do not incorporate forecasts of the future returns of equities (e.g., the S&P 500) as part of their pricing methodologies. Consequently, fixed-income can, and should, be used to support insurance products.

- *Third parties value insurance liabilities based upon the fixed-income market.*
  State regulators, taxing authorities, etc. value liabilities using fixed-income yields.

- *There is a significant implied opportunity cost for incremental*

equity-related investment reserves.
State regulators require insurance companies to hold aside
investment reserves [i.e., Asset Valuation Reserves (AVR)]
which cannot be used to "leverage up" the company's balance
sheet (e.g., support the sale of additional insurance products).
The incremental AVR for equities can approximate 30% (33%
for stocks versus 3% for fixed-income). When the company has
an average ROE of 20% for instance, the opportunity cost for
equities is 6% as shown below:

Incremental AVR		Average ROE		Opportunity Cost
30%	x	20%	=	6%

An opportunity cost of this magnitude exceeds the 5% equity risk
premium assumed by many investment professionals. Since there can be
little, if any, expected benefit associated with equities under these circumstances, it is difficult to justify assuming equity's historical return volatility.

WHAT IS THE ROLE OF FIXED-INCOME ASSETS?

Within the context of the **Need to Have** approach, fixed-income assets is
the asset class of choice. While operating within prescribed investment
guidelines, the role of fixed-income is:

- To immunize the liability and surplus against interest rate
  movements through dollar duration (Messmore (1990)).

- To generate appropriate returns required for "paying off" the
  economic liability.

The role of fixed income should be translated into a "normal portfolio"
or, in the language of the fixed-income market, a custom bond index (CBI).
The fixed-income market has much to learn from the equity market's
experience with normal portfolios. A CBI should reflect the liability as
well as the investment choices available to the manager.
Within the **Need to Have** approach, a CBI drives the asset allocation
process. It helps answer the question "What is the *minimum* amount of equities
required to fund the Economic Liability?" Conversely, "Can the fixed-income
market produce enough return to satisfy the Economic Liability?" The
following examples illustrate how a CBI can be used in this manner.

FIGURE 4
Example 1: Implementing "Need to Have" Approach

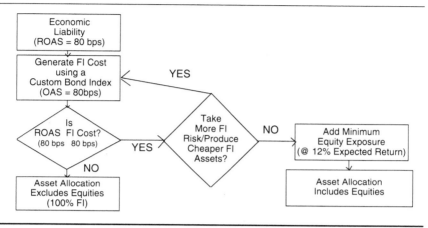

In the first example (Figure 4, above), an investor is able to earn enough return in the fixed-income market to fund the liabilities. The required option adjusted spread (ROAS) of the Economic Liability is 80 basis points, while the option adjusted spread (OAS) of a CBI is 80 basis points. Therefore, there is no need to assume equity exposure. (Note: The ROAS is calculated by identifying the spread over the spot curve which equates the market value of assets to the present value of the economic liability. Thus, it is somewhat akin to an IRR calculation.)

FIGURE 5
Example 2: Implementing "Need to Have Approach"

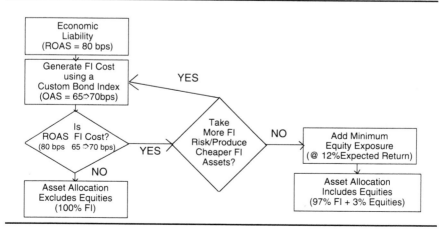

In the second example (Figure 5, above), an investor must purchase equities. The Economic Liability's ROAS is again 80 basis points, but in this case, the CBI's OAS is initially 65 basis points. The OAS of the CBI is increased to 70 basis points after private placements and other "cheaper" fixed-income assets are incorporated into the CBI. However, 70 basis points is still inadequate and equity exposure of 3% is required to fund the liabilities assuming a 12% expected return for equities.

Thus far, I have only discussed the use of a CBI within the context of the **Need to Have** approach for determining an equity allocation. The minimum equity requirement is arguably an important reference point. Investors with alternative approaches for allocating equities may want to apply the above process for this purpose. It is apparent that the CBI assumes a crucial position in the asset allocation decision process as well as in the ultimate management and measurement of the fixed-income portfolio. Characteristically, a CBI is:

- an immunized portfolio which provides

  a. instantaneous parallel yield curve shift protection through arbitrage free derived effective durations (Ho and Lee (1986)).

  b. instantaneous nonparallel yield curve *shift* protection through key rate durations (Ho (1990)).

  c. interest rate scenario protection through pathwise immunization/dedication and linear path space (Ho (1991)) while incorporating shortfall probability techniques (Liebowitz et al (1990)). This is particularly important for developing CBIs for interest sensitive liabilities such as single premium deferred annuities (SPDAs) (Norris and Epstein (1988)) and (Asay et al. (1989)).

- consistent with investment policy guidelines including acceptable names and dollar credit limits.

- comprised of existing and anticipated privately-sourced fixed-income asset positions as well as public bonds selected from a major third party index provider (e.g., Merrill Lynch, Lehman Brothers, etc.).

- optimization based, which is essential given the complexity and magnitude of the problem.

Thus, a reasonable approach for framing an optimization problem to construct a CBI could include:

	Rationale
Objective Function	
• Maximize Diversification	• An index should include as many bonds as possible.
	• Mitigates the "chasing" of mispriced bonds by minimizing, the aggregate perturbation of bonds' market value weights.
Assets Constraints	
• Effective Duration (EFF D) *(Eff D$_{Liability}$ ± "noise factor")*	Provides parallel yield curve shift protection.
• Key Rate Duration (KRD) *(KRD$_{Liability}$ ± "noise factor")*	Provides parallel yield curve shift protection.
• Shortfall Probability (SP) *(SP < x%)*	Provides specified interest rate scenarios protection.
• Convexity (C) *(C > x)*	Provides convexity protection.
• Sector Weights (SW) *(x% SW Y%)*	Consistent with market or investment policy guidelines.
• Purchase private placements *(Private Issue = x%)*	Forces solution to "buy" private placements in portfolio as a "core" holding since they will not likely be sold.
• Transaction Costs (TC) *(TC < $x)*	Places limits on transaction costs.

Using this objective function and a similar constraint set, I constructed the below CBI with an effective duration of 6.95 years by essentially reweighing the bonds in a large portfolio designed to replicate the Lehman Brothers Government/Corporate Index:

	Replicating Govt/Corp Portfolio	CBI	% Difference
Bonds	1144	831	<37%>
Effective Duration	4.70	6.95	48%
Sector Detail:			
• Treasury – %	69%	69%	–
– Duration	4.71	6.75	43%
• Corporate – %	24%	24%	–
– Duration	5.04	6.54	30%
• Agency – %	7%	7%	–
– Duration	4.05	10.83	167%

The number of bonds in the CBI decreased by only 37% while the effective duration increased by 48%. If one is uncomfortable with aspects of the CBI (e.g., the 10.83 effective duration of the Agency sector), a constraint can be added to the optimization to bring the solution within one's "comfort zone."

This CBI is objective in that it follows the "blind rule" of matching the sector allocations in the market. However, additional measures/indices are required particularly for performance attribution purposes. The need for multiple indices can most easily be seen with the following recommended approach for economic (i.e., TROR based) profitability measurement and performance attribution:

		Measurement Objectives
Portfolio TROR		
• Biased CBI TROR	Portfolio Management Gain	Identify value added by portfolio manager.
Biased CBI TROR		
• Objective CBI TROR	+ Investment Policy Gain	Identify value added by policy makers.
Objective CBI TROR		
• Liability TROR	+ Liability Translation Gain	Identify ability to translate liability cash flows into fixed income securities.
	Incremental Gross Profit	

Where:

Portfolio TROR = The total return of the actual fixed-income portfolio used to back a liability.

Biased CBI TROR = The total return of a fixed-income index constructed to incorporate senior management's market calls. Furthermore, the investment strategy reflected through the index is expected to produce returns which will satisfy the ROAS.

Objective CBI = The total return of fixed-income index is constructed to follow the "blind rule" of matching the market sector weights, average credit ratings, etc., while remaining key rate duration are matched to the liabilities. Unlike the biased CBI, the objective CBI does not *"reach"* for spread/returns.

Liability TROR = The total return of a liability cash flow discounted at treasury spot rates plus the ROAS. Although it captures changes in spot rates, the ROAS is fixed for a closed block of business and, thus, the Liability TROR does not attempt to capture changes in spreads in the fixed-income market.

Through some simple algebra, it is apparent that the aforementioned performance measurement formula can be reduced to:

Portfolio TROR – Liability TROR = Incremental Gross Profit

The ultimate objective is clearly to have the assets outperform the liabilities and is so captured in the formula. However, this reduction oversimplify the investment process and ignores the basic management tenet of matching authority with responsibility/accountability. For instance, the investment policy maker could have some excellent market calls (i.e., generated significant Investment Policy Gains) while the portfolio manager did a poor job with securities selection (i.e., generated significant Portfolio Management Losses). While these actions may have offset one another, it does not "tell the story" so corrective actions may be taken.

HOW SHOULD FIXED-INCOME ASSETS BE MANAGED?

A portfolio manager should manage fixed-income assets with his "eye on the ball." When the assets are tied to a liability, the "ball" should be a CBI.

When liabilities are translated into an index or benchmark, the traditional fixed-income investment management styles (of index replication, enhanced indexing and active management) become available to the portfolio manager. The biased CBI may be substituted for, the Salomon BIG, for example. As with the BIG, the portfolio manager should attempt to thoroughly understand the "enemy" (i.e., the Biased CBI) in terms of duration, convexity, sector, coupon, etc. breakdowns.

Furthermore, there is much need and interest in identifying an appropriate index for dedicated/immunized managers in general (Greer (1992)) and (Choie (1992)). The CBI approach described here incorporates the traditional tool of the dedicated/immunized portfolio manager (i.e., optimization, duration matching and convexity management). In addition, the CBI is consistent with the investment guidelines imposed upon the manager. Thus, the Biased CBI should be an acceptable benchmark for managers applying traditional dedicated/immunized portfolio management techniques.

CONCLUSION

Immunization is an extremely powerful theoretical concept. However, it was originally designed to "work" under some very restrictive conditions (e.g., for instantaneous parallel yield curve shifts only). Nonetheless, immunization forms the basis of asset/liability management as it is generally practiced today.

The use of a CBI enhances the immunization process through more effective asset/liability management performance attribution and asset allocation.

Asset/liability management is enhanced by providing nonparallel yield curve shift protection through key rate durations. Further, the incorporation of pathwise immunization seeks to make the market value surplus immune to specified interest rate change *over time* (i.e., interest-rate scenarios) while having the assets outperform the liability on a TROR basis.

Performance attribution is enhanced by the separate identification by the portfolio manager and the investment policy makers of the value added. Moreover, it is now possible to identify whether the portfolio manager took advantage of the changes in the market, in addition to the traditional performance measures of immunized bond portfolio managers (Ho and Lee (1986)).

Asset allocation is enhanced by the ability to identify the minimum of equity assets required to satisfy the economic liability under the **Need to Have** approach.

NOTES

1. A high percentage of the present value of a given liability can be attributed to cash flows beyond 30 years.
2. The change in equity market value is unreliable for an instantaneous, small and parallel shift of the yield curve, the traditional measure of immunization. The result of this unreliability is the limited immunization value of equity within this context.

REFERENCES

Asay, Michael R., Peter J. Bouyoucos, and Anthony M. Marciano, 1989, An economic approach to valuation of single premium deferred annuities, Goldman Sachs Publication.

Choie, Kenneth, 1992, Caveats in immunization of pension liabilities, *Journal of Portfolio Management* Winter, 54-69.

Greer, Boyce I., 1992, Market-oriented benchmarks for immunized portfolios, *Journal of Portfolio Management* Spring, 26-35.

Ho, T.S.Y., and Lee, S.B., 1986, Term structure movements and pricing interest rate contingent claims, *Journal of Finance* 41, 1011-1029.

Ho, T.S.Y., 1990, Key rate durations: A measure of interest rate risks exposure, Working Paper, Salomon Brothers Center.

Ho, T.S.Y., 1991, Managing illiquid bonds and the linear path space, Working Paper, Salomon Brothers Center.

Liebowitz, Martin L., Lawrence N. Bader, and Stanley Kogelman, 1990, Asset allocation under liability uncertainty, Salomon Brothers Publication.

Messmore, Thomas E., 1990, The duration of surplus, *Journal of Portfolio Management* Winter, 19-22.

Norris, Peter D. and Sheldon Epstein, 1988, Finding the immunizing investment for insurance liabilities: The case of the SPDA, Morgan Stanley Publication.

Reddington, F.M., 1952, Review of the principles of life-office valuations, *Journal of the Institute of Actuaries* 18, 286-340.

Yoon, Young W., 1992, A practical approach to asset allocation, *Fixed-Income Portfolio Management: Issues and Solutions* (Dow Jones-Irwin, Homewood, IL).

CHAPTER 7

A PRACTICAL APPROACH TO ASSET ALLOCATION

Young W. Yoon, Ph.D
Senior Vice President, Equitable Capital Management Corporation

INTRODUCTION

This chapter discusses some of the problems large financial institutions or pension funds face in making asset allocation decisions. Asset allocation has received a great deal of attention in both the academic and business communities.[1] The topic encompasses three types of asset allocation: strategic, tactical and dynamic. Strategic asset allocation, is concerned with the long-term target asset mix. As such, it is based on long-term forecasts and broad historical analyses of how capital markets perform. Tactical asset allocation, on the other hand, is a short-term strategy which seeks return enhancement by shifting the asset mix of a portfolio in response to market conditions. Dynamic asset allocation shifts asset mix, not based on a forecast of short-term beliefs, but based on changing market conditions in order to control downside risk.

While all three types of asset allocations are utilized in practice, by far the most emphasis has been placed on strategic asset allocation. Even tactical asset allocation, which is growing in importance, starts with the targets arrived at in strategic asset allocation as a base and then modifies this base solution. In this chapter, we will concentrate on strategic asset allocation, although our analysis will have implications for both tactical and dynamic asset allocation.

Young W. Yoon, Ph.D. is Senior Vice President, Equitable Capital Management Corporation, 1285 Avenue of the Americas, New York, New York, 10019

FIGURE 1
Asset Allocation Process
Surplus Maximization

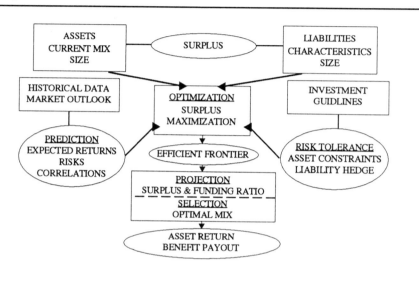

This chapter will describe the key elements in the asset allocation process. But first, we will establish the need to include liabilities in the allocation decision and the effect this has on the firm's objective function. We will show that if you attempt to optimize the asset mix without considering the nature of the liabilities, the result can be a portfolio which is completely inappropriate.

In the first section of this chapter, we show that the inclusion of liabilities is important and that this leads to a natural formulation of the portfolio problem in terms of a net worth or surplus concept. Having established this, we proceed with an analysis of the asset allocation process. The asset allocation process is represented diagrammatically in Figure 1. The key elements in this diagram are described in the remainder of this chapter. In the section entitled *Developing Capital Market Assumptions*, we describe alternative methods for arriving at capital market forecasts. Assumptions about the future are a key part of any allocation procedure. Data on liabilities, which is an important asset allocation process, receives special treatment in this section. The next section, *Solving for the Efficient Frontier*, deals with solving for efficient combinations (the efficient frontier) of assets and liabilities. The section on *Projecting Surplus Levels* discusses the very difficult problem of choosing one combination of assets from a variety of efficient asset mixes. The solution involves incorporating management risk tolerance into the decision process and examining possible results over a multihorizon setting. Let us now turn to a discussion of the importance of the surplus framework for the investment decision problem.

IMPORTANCE OF THE SURPLUS FRAMEWORK

There are two analytical frameworks for the investment decision-making process. The first examines trade-offs between the mean and variance of yearly returns for the assets invested in the portfolio. By focusing solely on assets, this framework attempts to maximize asset returns and implicitly expects that the accumulated assets will meet the future liability. The second framework examines the tradeoffs between asset returns and liability returns on net worth (assets minus liabilities). To examine why the mean and variance of yearly returns on net worth or surplus is an appropriate asset allocation framework for most investment decisons, we will consider two examples, insurance companies and pension funds.[2]

Let us first consider insurance companies. Why should insurance companies care about year by year changes in net worth rather than net worth at some point in the future? First, while existing liabilities may terminate at some point in the future, as time passes, new liabilities are added and the firm hopes that this process will continue indefinitely into the future. Thus, the maturity of the existing liabilities do not provide a natural date at which to examine investment performance. Second, regulators examine year by year changes in net worth or surplus to determine the amount of new business the firm can engage in. In fact, a company with negative net worth is insolvent even though the firm's investment policy might subsequently result in positive net worth. These considerations explain why an insurance company should care about return on net worth rather than return on assets.

Another example of an investment situation where a manager should focus on changes in net worth is the pension fund. The liabilities for the pension fund may well terminate at some future date. This has suggested to some that analysis of net worth at this date might be appropriate, and a number of services have been developed to aid asset allocation based on this premise. However, year by year, changes in net worth do have an impact on the firm. Current accounting standards (FASB) call for assets and liabilities to be recorded at market value and prescribe procedures to deal with a shortfall in assets relative to liabilities. In particular, a sufficient shortfall in assets relative to liabilities results in additional payments to the fund from the corporation and must be reflected in the income statement of the corporation sponsoring the pension fund. In addition, the Omnibus Budget Reconciliation Act of 1987 (OBRA) mandates a focus on surplus through an additional insurance premium if the funding ratio falls below 125%. These considerations explain why pension funds should focus on net worth rather than return on assets.

Concentrating only on the asset side, as a number of asset allocation programs do, can hide the true risk return characteristics of an asset to an investor. Liabilities are usually valued as if they were bond payments. It is usually argued that to find the current value of the liabilities we discount at the appropriate interest rate. Since the value of one class of assets — debt — is also dependent on the level of interest rates, changes in value of liabilities and debt are highly correlated. If we focus on the return on assets, we may ignore the hedging characteristics of debt instruments, which indicate that low returns for debt will also be likely at times when the market value of the liabilities is reduced.

On the other hand, equities — another class of assets — are likely to be reasonably unrelated to changes in the value of liabilities. Defined pension plans with a cost of living adjustment represent another example of the importance of focusing on returns on net worth, rather than assets only for pension plans. Consider two assets with the same volatility, but one asset's return depends on changes in inflation while the second asset's return is unaffected by inflation. An examination of the variability of return on assets suggests that the assets are equally risky. However, the asset whose return is affected by inflation has very desirable hedge characteristics that are ignored unless liabilities are an explicit part of the planning process.

For all the above reasons, the return on net worth is the appropriate investment criteria for many investment problems.

DEVELOPING CAPITAL MARKET ASSUMPTIONS

The optimal asset mix, given the liability stream, depends critically on the expected returns of each asset class; the volatility of returns for each asset class; and the correlations between returns of the asset classes with each other and with the liabilities. In this section we will discuss how these estimates can be made.

FIGURE 2
Description of Asset Classes

VARIABLE	DESCRIPTION
Common Stocks	S&P 500 Index/Ibbotson Associates Data
Active Stocks	Separate Account 4 of Equitable Capital
Small Stocks	DFA Small Co. Fund/Ibbotson Associates
Global Stocks	Morgan Stanley EAFE Index
Convertible Bonds	Value Line Convertible Bond Index
High-Yield Bonds	Salomon Brothers' High Yield Bond Index
Long Bonds	Lehman Brothers' Long Govt/Corp Index
Intermediate Bonds	Lehman Brothers' Intermediate Govt/Corp Index
MBS	Lehman Brothers' MBS Index
T-Bills	T-Bill Index/Ibbotson Associates Data
Real Estate	NACREIT Index
CPI	Consumer Price Index

Historically, predictions of capital market conditions began by analyzing historical experience and then examining how current conditions modify that experience. For each asset class we would like to find an index or portfolio which has the same return distribution as we would expect to achieve if we invest in that asset class. Generally, we have a choice of using the returns on a managed portfolio or on an index. Many indices are matched by passive managers and can be viewed as a proxy for a passive portfolio. If our managers' behavior does not deviate dramatically from the indices' characteristics (e.g. average duration or beta) then using an index is probably the better choice since we are likely to have a much longer history to examine. If, on the other hand, the managers we select have performance characteristics dramatically different from the index, then using the historical return pattern of the managed funds would most likely be the preferred choice. The asset classes we use in our asset allocation analysis and the source of the data are shown in Figure 2. Some of the trade-offs we made are apparent from the table. For example, we use Lehman Brothers Bond indices because their duration is much closer to the duration on our active portfolios than is the duration of the Ibbotson indices. Similarly, we use the active stock account because its performance deviates significantly from the market indices we could have chosen.

FIGURE 3
Historical Asset Returns and Risks (Annualized Figures in Percents)

Period	Rate of Return					Standard Deviations				
	4/76-3/81	4/81-3/86	4/86-3/91	1565 Year	4/76-Year**	4/81-3/81	4/86-3/86	15 3/91	65 Year	Year**
Common Stock	12.28	18.48	15.32	15.31	12.10	13.89	13.81	18.62	15.63	20.8
Active Stock	18.72	19.55	17.03	18.41	17.29	17.45	23.72	19.73		
Small Stock	34.33	20.48	5.61	19.63	17.10	23.14	16.28	20.85	20.44	35.4
Global Stock	16.21	22.44	16.43	18.32	13.61	16.65	22.10	17.86		
Convertible Bond	26.19	4.84	13.66*		11.95	12.85	12.75*			
High Yield	29.33	7.89	11.90*		5.89	8.54	8.35*			
Intermediate Bond	6.04	16.46	8.42	10.21	5.10	6.20	5.71	3.70	5.45	5.50
Long Bond	2.18	22.91	8.54	10.90	5.50	10.84	13.14	8.36	11.23	8.40
MBS	3.66	20.07	10.26	11.16	10.70	12.11	4.81	9.93		
Real Estate	15.12	12.09	6.35	11.14	1.56	1.13	0.55	1.50		
T-Bill	8.21	9.95	6.77	8.31	3.70	0.87	0.74	0.37	0.77	3.40
CPI	9.73	4.23	4.41	6.06	3.20	1.07	1.11	0.80	1.21	4.70

*10-Year Data
**Ibbotson Data

FIGURE 4
Historical Return Correlation
15 Year

	Stocks	Active Stocks	Small Stocks	Global Stocks	Intmd Bonds	Long Bonds	MBS	Real Estate	T-Bill	CPI
Stocks	1.00	0.95	0.82	0.43	0.31	0.36	0.30	-0.03	-0.08	-0.14
Active Stocks		1.00	0.82	0.36	0.23	0.29	0.24	0.03	-0.07	-0.12
Small Stocks			1.00	0.35	0.21	0.24	0.20	0.02	-0.10	-0.08
Global Stocks				1.00	0.20	0.22	0.17	-0.04	-0.15	-0.23
Intermediate Bonds					1.00	0.95	0.92	-0.14	0.17	-0.19
Long Bonds						1.00	0.91	-0.19	0.06	-0.26
Mortgages							1.00	-0.16	0.08	-0.20
Real Estate								1.00	0.50	0.41
T-Bills									1.00	0.38
CPI										1.00

We examined historical experience to gain insight into future risk/ return relationship. There is extensive empirical evidence that the historical risk structure is predictive of the future (See Elton and Gruber (1973), Eun and Resnick (1984), and Elton, Gruber and Urich (1978)). Although it may be less applicable to an individual security, at the portfolio level, historical experience is a good predictor of the future. Figures 3 and 4 show for a series of asset classes, the expected return, standard deviations, and correlations of return over the fifteen-year period of April 1976 to March 1991, three five-year subperiods, and, where data was available, since 1926. Note that the standard deviations and correlations, while not identical in each five-year period, are highly related. It is the relative level that affects asset allocation. Note that the relative size of the standard deviation across asset classes is even more stable than the level itself. Thus, we feel historical experience plus judgment can provide accurate estimates of the risk structure.

However, as Figure 3 shows, historical average realized return is a poor guide for future expected return, as demonstrated by the average realized return for small stocks in each five-year period. Thus, in order to estimate expected return we utilize a risk premium approach. The risk premium on an asset class is estimated by taking the difference in two different return series. The common stock risk premium, for example, represents the average additional return earned by investors for taking the incremental risk of stocks relative to treasury bills.

FIGURE 5
Estimation of Risk Premium
Risk Premia for Five Different Periods

Spread Relation	4/76-3/81	4/81-3/86	4/86-3/91	15 Year	65 Year	Premium Estimates
T-Bill/CPI	-1.5	5.7	2.4	2.3	0.5	2.0
Stock/T-Bill	4.1	8.5	8.5	7.0	8.4	7.0
Active S/Stock	6.4	1.1	1.7	3.1		1.5
Small S/Stock	22.1	2.0	- 9.7	4.3	5.0	2.0
Global S/Stock	3.9	3.9	1.1	3.0		2.0
Conv Bd/Stock		7.7	- 10.5	1.7		1.5
High Yield/Long Bd		6.4	- 0.7	1.0		1.5
Inter Bd/T-Bill	-2.2	6.5	0.1	0.7	0.4	0.7
Long Bd/Inter Bond	-3.8	6.5	0.1	0.7	0.4	0.7
MBS/Inter Bd	1.5	3.6	1.8	1.4		1.0
Real Est/CPI	5.3	7.8	1.9	5.1		3.0

FIGURE 6
Premium Estimation
Economic Recovery Periods

	Average of Two Slow Recovery Periods	Entire Recovery Period	Premium Estimates
T-Bill/CPI	0.4	2.4	1.5
Stock/T-Bill	5.5	7.7	7.5
Small S/Stock	8.8	6.5	7.0
Global/Stock	-8.0	-0.5	0.0
Inter Bd/T-Bill	2.5	3.2	2.5
Long Bd/Inter Bd	1.7	-0.0	0.7
Real Est/CPI	1.8	7.5	4.5

We started our risk premium analysis by first examining historical risk premiums. These are shown in Figure 5 for the same set of five, fifteen and sixty-five-year periods used previously. The principal feature of Figure 5 is the great variability in risk premiums across time. For example, the small stock premium varies from plus 22.1 to minus 9.7. In order to effectively estimate expected returns we need to understand what causes these variations. Since risk/returns are related to economic conditions in terms of growth, we divided historical periods not by time but by level of economic growth, inflation and interest rates. At the time of this study, the economy was characterized by low interest rates, low inflation, and economic recovery. Figure 6 shows the premium over two similar historical periods characterized by slow economic recovery, and the premium over the entire recovery period. The last column shows the estimates we used given the premia in these two periods, premia in other periods and our judgment about the future.

For many asset classes, the premia changed very little over periods of similar economic conditions. For example, intermediate bonds premia ranged from 1.8 to 3.2. Small stocks and global stocks were the exception. In the case of global stocks, varied economic conditions across countries and changes in exchange rates explain most of the variance. For these asset classes, forecasts of these variables must be taken into account. Expected return is by far the most difficult input to estimate. However, a structured approach should improve the process.

In the surplus framework, the liabilities are as important as assets and their returns need to be forecasted. Liabilities can be viewed as a stream of payments very similar to a bond. For retired employees of a large company with a fixed pension plan, these cash flows are highly predictable. The primary determinant of their current value is interest rate. Thus, this class of pension liabilities are highly sensitive to interest rates. For a plan with COLA inflation has a significant impact on liabilities. These characteristics must be explicitly modeled to accurately estimate correlations between asset returns and changes in the value of liabilities and to ensure consistent return forecasts for assets and liabilities under different economic scenarios.

Because the actuarial estimates of the growth in additional liabilities was unrelated to reasonable changes in economic scenarios in our study, we considered it to be exogenous. The only endogenous factor effecting the present value of liabilities was the interest rate. The duration of the liabilities closely matched the long-term bond index. Thus, we used our estimate of the standard deviation of the long-term bond index as the standard deviation of the liabilities and the correlation of the long bond index with other assets as the correlation of liabilities with other assets. If we had not been so fortuitous, we would adjust the characteristics of the index chosen as a proxy for liabilities to reflect the difference in the duration of liabilities from the duration of the bond index.

SOLVING FOR THE EFFICIENT FRONTIER

Once we have prepared input parameters (such as expected returns and risk characteristics for each asset class), the next step is to solve for optimal asset mixes. The procedure is a standard quadratic programming problem. Liabilities are treated as a short position of an asset class. A constraint is placed on the proportion invested in the liability to insure that the liability is a part of the optimal portfolio.[3]

One of the considerations at this point is whether upper and lower bond constraints should be placed on investments in different asset classes. Lower bound constraints arise because part of the assets which are currently invested (in real estate, for example) may be sufficiently illiquid that, at least initially, one does not want to sell the assets. A second reason for a lower bound constraint is potential contractual obligations with external managers. Upper bound constraints are really risk controls.

Ideally, if all estimates were accurate, the output from the quadratic programming procedure would be sufficient and serve as a risk control tool. We used Bill Sharpe's Asset Allocation algorithm to produce a mean variance efficient frontier for surplus. A typical output is shown in Figure 7. To see the difference in using return on assets compared to return on net worth examine columns A and E in Figure 7. The three rows at the bottom of the table show the return on assets. Note that the portfolio under column E has a higher mean return than the portfolio in column A (13.87 compared to 10.80) and a lower risk (11.7% compared to 12.73). Under the asset-only framework, we would say portfolio A is dominated and eliminate it from consideration. However, when we concentrate on surplus as shown on the top three rows of Figure 7, we reach a different conclusion. Column E has both a higher mean return and a higher risk. Both are potential candidates for inclusion.

FIGURE 7
Efficient Asset Mixes

	Current	A	B	C	D	E	F	G	H	I	J
SURPLUS:											
Expected return	16.88	14.34	17.92	21.83	26.43	31.07	37.55	44.28	53.61	59.47	63.19
Std deviation	34.95	27.78	30.08	33.90	39.42	45.54	55.21	66.28	82.66	93.45	100.48
Risk coefficient	2.07	1.94	1.68	1.55	1.49	1.47	1.47	1.50	1.54	1.57	1.59
ASSETS:											
Stocks	20.61	10.00	10.00	10.00	10.00	10.00	10.00	10.00	10.00	10.00	10.00
Sml Stox	0.00	0.00	2.63	4.78	6.82	9.05	17.26	25.51	37.41	45.10	50.00
T-Bill	0.50	0.00	0.00	0.00	0.00	0.00	0.00	0.00	0.00	0.00	0.00
Inter Bnd	0.90	0.00	0.00	0.00	0.00	0.00	0.00	0.00	0.00	0.00	0.00
Long Bnd	68.00	70.00	70.00	70.00	60.91	50.99	41.09	22.13	10.00	10.00	10.00
Mortgages	0.00	20.00	9.18	0.00	0.00	0.00	1.66	12.35	12.59	4.90	0.00
High Yld	1.71	0.00	8.19	12.69	15.67	19.96	20.00	20.00	20.00	20.00	20.00
Conv Bnd	0.00	0.00	0.00	0.00	0.00	0.00	0.00	0.00	0.00	0.00	0.00
FRC	0.00	0.00	0.00	0.00	0.00	0.00	0.00	0.00	0.00	0.00	0.00
FARM	0.00	0.00	0.00	0.00	0.00	0.00	0.00	0.00	0.00	0.00	0.00
SA8	8.29	0.00	0.00	0.00	0.00	0.00	0.00	0.00	0.00	0.00	0.00
EAFE	0.00	0.00	0.00	2.53	6.59	10.00	10.00	10.00	10.00	10.00	10.00
Glob Bnd	0.00	0.00	0.00	0.00	0.00	0.00	0.00	0.00	0.00	0.00	0.00
PORTFOLIO:											
Expected return	11.26	10.80	11.45	12.17	13.01	13.87	15.06	16.29	18.00	19.08	19.76
Std deviation	11.62	12.73	12.27	12.09	11.87	1.70	12.41	13.27	15.40	17.15	18.31
Risk coefficient	1.03	1.18	1.07	0.99	0.91	0.84	0.82	0.81	0.86	0.90	0.93

The main difference in the asset holdings between columns A and E is the inclusion of high yield debt and small stocks in column E and the corresponding reduction in long bonds and mortgages from column A.

Looking at return on assets, this appears to reduce risk.

Stocks and high-yield debt have less correlation with long bonds than mortgages or other long bonds on themselves. However, long bonds and mortgages as a group are more highly correlated with liabilities than is a combination of stock and high-yield bonds. Thus, replacing long-term bonds and mortgages with stocks and high-yield debt increases the risk on the surplus. Using return on assets rather than return on surplus as a decision criteria, leads to opposite conclusions concerning the risk of replacing some of the government bonds and mortgages with high-yield debt and stock. The output of the quadratic program as we formulate it shows the optimal asset mix at different risk and return level for the surplus. The optimal portfolio depends on the risk tolerance of the managers involved.

This decision is rarely made explicit. Most managers find that reviewing the consequences of their choices aids their decision process. This is the subject of the next section.

PROJECTING THE SURPLUS LEVELS

To aid the manager in making a choice among different optimal portfolios, it is often useful to simulate what level of surplus would be attained if a particular asset choice were made, and return forecasts were accurate. Surplus levels can be directly forecast using the expected return and standard direction of the return from the quadratic programming problem. Figure 8 shows the output of the simulation for the quadratic programming results shown in Figure 7. These are surplus figures projected for one to five years into the future. The figure in the table represents the average surplus level, the 10% and 90% probability levels. For example, for asset allocation C the expected surplus level in five years is 109.14 or higher, and 90% of the time it is greater than 11.98.

FIGURE 8
Growth in Surplus

Probability:	Current	One-Year Horizon									
		A	B	C	D	E	F	G	H	I	J
10-HIGH	61.67	49.94	56.48	65.28	76.95	89.44	108.31	129.23	159.56	179.25	191.98
50-EXPECTED	16.88	14.34	17.92	21.83	26.43	31.07	37.55	44.28	53.61	59.47	63.19
90-LOW	-27.91	-21.26	-20.64	-21.62	-24.10	-27.31	-33.21	-40.67	-52.33	-60.31	-65.60
Prob. of increasing surplus	68.44	69.85	72.57	73.89	74.86	75.17	75.17	74.86	74.22	73.89	73.57

(continued on next page)

Three-Year Horizon

Probability:	Current	A	B	C	D	E	F	G	H	I	J
10-HIGH	128.21	104.68	120.55	140.75	166.79	194.30	235.22	279.97	344.34	385.86	412.65
50-EXPECTED	50.63	43.01	53.76	65.49	79.28	93.20	112.66	132.83	160.84	178.40	189.58
90-LOW	-26.95	-18.65	-13.02	-9.77	-8.24	-7.91	-9.91	-14.31	-22.65	-29.07	-33.50
Prob. of increasing surplus	79.95	81.33	84.85	86.86	87.70	88.10	88.10	87.70	86.86	86.43	86.21

Five-Year Horizon

Probability:	Current	A	B	C	D	E	F	G	H	I	J
10-HIGH	184.55	151.29	175.82	206.30	245.11	285.85	345.98	411.35	504.96	565.17	603.95
50-EXPECTED	84.39	71.69	89.60	109.14	132.13	155.33	187.76	221.39	268.07	297.33	315.96
90-LOW	-15.76	-7.91	3.38	11.98	19.15	24.80	29.53	31.43	31.18	29.49	27.97
Prob. of increasing surplus	85.99	87.49	90.82	92.51	93.32	93.70	93.57	93.19	92.65	92.22	92.07

Recasting the table in Figure 7 often helps managers to make better decisions. Expressing surplus as a funding ratios (surplus plus assets over liabilities) is often helpful. Similarly, calculating the probability of having surplus which requires additional funding is useful in making choices between alternative portfolios

CONCLUSION

This chapter reviews the major steps in the asset allocation decision and discusses some of the major problems in strategic asset allocation. While some judgment will always be necessary for estimating asset returns and selecting the best allocation from a larger number of good choices, we have made real progress in specifying the steps of the process. The framework we propose has been successfully implemented at Equitable for several years. Its success, is due in part to a combination of management interaction in selecting optimal mixes, with the input of data within a well-structured model.

As we have shown above, the incorporation of liabilities is necessary to realize an optimal solution. While we have made a significant first step in incorporating liabilities, we are still left with one problem. We have treated the amount of liabilities as a fixed quantity. In fact, the size of liabilities as well as the timing and return is uncertain. Also, many of the influences which effect the returns on assets (e.g. changes in interest into changes in cost of living) also effect the size of liabilities of an institution. At this time, we are in the process of analyzing this added complexity.

NOTES

1. See for example Arnott and Fabozzi (1988) for an excellent compilation of papers on asset allocation. Also see Arnott and Bernstein (1988) and Black and Litterman (1991).

2. See Liebowitz, Bader and Kogelman (1992) for additional support of this criteria.

3. If there are unfunded liabilities, the present value of future funding plans needs to be included or the procedure will lead to extreme risk taking. Or, a simulation procedure could be used to examine alternative investment plans.

REFERENCES

Arnott, Robert, and Peter Bernstein, 1988, The right way to manage your pension fund, *Harvard Business Review* Jan-Feb, 95-102

Arnott, Robert and Frank Fabozzi, 1988, *Asset Allocation* (Probus Publishing Company, Chicago, Illinois).

Black, Fischer and Robert Litterman, 1991, Asset allocation: combining investor views with market equilibrium, *Journal of Fixed-Income Management* Sept., 7-18.

Elton, Edwin, Martin Gruber and Thomas Urich, 1978, Are betas best? *Journal of Finance* Vol. XIII, No 5, 1375-1384.

Elton, Edwin and Martin Gruber, 1973, Estimating the dependence structure of share prices-implications for portfolio selection, *Journal of Finance* Vol. VII,I No. 5, 1203-1232.

Eun, Cheol and Bruce Resnick, 1984, Estimating the correlation structure of international share prices, *Journal of Finance* Vol. 39 No. 5, 1311-1324.

Fein, Donald and Robert Stanbough, 1986, Predicting return in the stock and bond markets, *Journal of Financial Economics* 17, 357-390.

French, Kenneth, William G. Schwert and Albert Stanbough, 1987, Expected stock returns and volatility, *Journal of Financial Economics* 19, 3-29.

Liebowitz, Martin, Lawrence Bader and Stanley Kogelman, 1992, Asset allocation under liability uncertainty, Salomon Brothers.

Sharpe, William, 1987, An algorithm for portfolio improvement, in Kenneth Lawrence, John and Gary Reeves, *Advances in Mathematical Programming and Financial Planning,* Vol. 1, 155-170 (AI Press, Greenwich).

Sharpe, William, 1992, Asset allocation management style and performance measurement, *Journal of Portfolio Management* Winter, 7-19.

Sharpe, William and Lawrence Tint, 1990, Liabilities: a new approach, *Journal of Portfolio Management* Winter, 5-10.

CHAPTER 8

USING SIMULATION MODELS TO IMPROVE INSURANCE COMPANY PERFORMANE

Thomas A. McAvity, Jr.,
Vice President, Quantitative Research,
Lincoln National Investment Management Company

INTRODUCTION

In making decisions, insurers are often too heavily influenced by the quest for growth in premium revenue and in-force business, by the desire to improve short-term results, and by the need to comply with the expectations of regulators, rating agencies, and other constituents. Product and investment strategies are not sufficiently integrated.

This chapter describes how insurance companies can use simulation models to improve the quality of strategic and operating decisions and, hence, long-run corporate performance. It attempts to bridge the gap

Thomas A. McAvity, Jr. is Vice President, Quantitative Research, Lincoln National Investment Management Company, P.O. Box 1110, 1300 South Clinton Street, Fort Wayne, IN, 46801.

The author would like to thank Tom Ho for helpful ideas and other comments throughout the development of this chapter. He would also like to acknowledge the many valuable insights given to him by colleagues at Lincoln National Corporation, particularly from David Becker, Dennis Blume, Jon Boscia, Gary Cooper, Luke Girard, Steve Lewis, Rich Klein, Gary McPhail, Reed Miller, Dick Robertson, and Mike Zurcher. Finally, he would like to thank fellow students of asset-liability management and investment strategy outside Lincoln National Corporation–Michael Asay, David Babbel, Shane Chalke, Sheldon Epstein, Vince Kaminski, Stan Kogelman, Bob Lally, Marty Leibowitz, Bob Litterman, Jeff Margolis, Peter Noris, Bill Panning, Mike Siegel, Robert Stricker, Jim Tilley, Dave Tyson, Fred Weinberger, Larry Weiss, and Young Yoon.

The opinions presented in this chapter are solely those of the author and do not represent the policies or views of Lincoln National Corporation.

between the techniques of operations research and financial economics and the practice of corporate management, strategy formulation, and operational decision-making.

Simulation should be used to evaluate current strategies and to devise better strategies, taking uncertainty explicitly into account by using a suitable sample of scenarios. If simulation is to contribute effectively to performance, it must be more than a well-developed laboratory tool; it must be driven by the realities of the business, with active participation by line executives, and its results must be integrated into decision processes.

This chapter is organized as follows:

The first section, *Economic Framework,* outlines the economic role of insurance companies as bearers of risks for customers and as investment and risk intermediaries. It considers the economic and corporate strategy implications of economies of scale, diversification of risk, and the long horizon required for measuring risk and return from alternative business strategies and resource commitments.

The second section, *Recommended Analytic Framework*, proposes a more formal statement of the analytical framework within which simulation should be applied. Insurers must meet the expectations of regulators, rating agencies, and stakeholders. Policies currently followed by many insurers suggest an imbalance in favor of maximizing growth and pleasing constituents over the short run. The proposed framework for decision-making is to maximize the "risk-adjusted build-up" of economic value over a five to ten-year horizon subject to the constraints imposed by government regulations and the expectations of constituents. The risk-adjusted build-up of economic value can be summarized as the expected net present value of the utility of cash flows to the horizon and the terminal value, with the expectation taken across a suitable sample of scenarios. The utility function should be consistent with the long-run interests and risk aversion of stakeholders, as interpreted by management and the board of directors.

The third section, *Decisions at the Activity Level,* considers asset-liability management at the level of the individual business activity. Existing decision processes are guided too often by short-term performance measurement systems, using accounting data that fails to capture the long-run effects of current period decisions. Our recommendations center around the simulation of results over a suitably long period to test the relative appeal of alternative state-contingent, adaptive decision rules. After illustrating simulation with a simple example, we recommend using a variety of simulation techniques to financially engineer strategies that will produce a more desirable profile of results across a carefully selected sample of scenarios.

The fourth section, *The Corporate Level*, describes how the scenario results achieved at the line-of-business level can be rolled up to the level of the regulated insurance company and the holding company. It describes an iterative, top-down and bottom-up process of rebalancing activity levels within the corporate portfolio and improving activity strategies such that the corporation's composite strategy will generate a more desirable profile of results, taking all sources of risk and their cross-correlations into account.

The final section, *Implementation*, considers how the benefits of these analytic techniques can be integrated into existing decision processes, notwithstanding the presence of cultural obstacles to change.

ECONOMIC FRAMEWORK: DECISIONS THAT DRIVE CORPORATE PERFORMANCE

Activities

An insurer's operations can be divided into building blocks called *activities*. We can then examine decisions at the activity level, the corporate "portfolio" level, and intermediate levels of aggregation selected as relevant for decision-making purposes (e.g., activities which use a costly common resource such as a sales force.) The allocation of capital to activities and to costly resources is a key corporate strategy decision.

Each activity should be a more or less self-contained element of the business, in the same spirit as the concept of "strategic business unit" employed in corporate planning. An activity might typically entail the sale of a product or homogeneous product line to a particular market or market segment through a particular distribution channel. Activities typically generate investable funds, and the strategy for investing such funds is an integral part of the business strategy for the activity.

Each of the activities conducted by insurance companies can be broken down into four common elements:

1. *Selling risk-bearing products*: Allowing a customer to transfer risk, e.g., of mortality, morbidity or casualty. The availability of reinsurance allows insurance companies to function as *risk intermediaries* as well as *risk portfolio companies.*

2. *Selling investment products*: Providing customized and

sometimes tax-advantaged products for capital accumulation, annuitization, and liquidity. In selling variable products, insurers act as *agents*. In selling guaranteed or fixed products, insurers function as *investment intermediaries*.

3. *Delivering processing services:* Processing claims, benefit payments, and records, with the goal of providing a desired quality of service at least cost.

4. *Investing*: It is useful to divide the investment process into two parts, a) the systematic investment strategy engineered to support the cash flows required for claims and benefits for each activity and b) the overlay of active asset allocation and investment management on top of those systematic strategies. In this deco-position, the second part is isolated as *investment arbitrage*.

Diversification of Risks

For now, let us define risk in terms of underperforming a minimum standard of return on equity over an appropriate time interval. Diversification reduces the effective total risk assumed by insurers in three ways. First, aggregate risk is reduced by diversification of exposures to uncorrelated or weakly correlated sources of systematic risk like interest rates, asset default rates and mortality. Second, two activities may have mutually hedging exposures to a source of systematic risk (e.g., broad increases in mortality rates hurt term life and help on-benefit annuities). Third, diversification of nonsystematic risk reduces effective risk through the law of large numbers, (e.g., in insuring mortality for 100,000 lives or accepting company-specific default in a bond portfolio equally weighted among 500 corporate obligors.)

FIGURE 1
Probability (Portfolio Return < 0%)

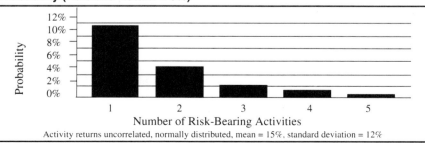

Number of Risk-Bearing Activities

Activity returns uncorrelated, normally distributed, mean = 15%, standard deviation = 12%

The first type of risk reduction is illustrated by Figure 1, which assumes that an insurer may allocate a fixed amount of capital equally to a portfolio of one, two, three, four, or five activities. By assumption, each activity is exposed to a single source of risk, and these risks are mutually uncorrelated. Each activity has an expected return of 15% with a standard deviation of 12%. Figure 1 shows the probability that the return will be less than 0% (i.e., a loss) for each of the five alternative portfolios. As the number of uncorrelated risk-bearing activities is increased, the probability of a loss drops sharply.

The capacity to bear risk is a function of capital. Evolving risk-based capital models used by regulators and rating agencies assess whether an insurer's exposures to risk are excessive in relation to statutory surplus. Some insurers also develop more accurate internal measures of required capital to cover adverse future experience, as described in Zurcher (1991).

Figure 1 implies that a corporate strategy which puts equal weighting on each of five activities is more efficient (in that it requires less capital and has a lower probability of underperforming) than one which conducts only one activity. With a given amount of capital, an insurer can conduct a larger volume of activity and generate more premiums and more profits with a diversified strategy than with an undiversified strategy.

FIGURE 2
Aggregate Risk Exposures Across Lines of Business

	INTEREST RATES	ASSET DEFAULTS	MORTALITY	PROPERTY CASUALTY
GICS & PENSION B/O	XXX	XXX		
DEFERED ANNUITIES	XXX	XXX		
PROPERTY CASUALTY	XX	XX		XXX
UNIVERSAL LIFE	XX	XX	XXX	
LIFE REINSURANCE	X	X	XXX	
COMPOSITE	XXX	XXX	XX	XX

Figure 2 illustrates how the risk exposures of several life and property-casualty lines might be rolled up to reveal the effective aggregate exposures of the corporate portfolio. In this stylized and over-simplified example, some risks, like interest rates, are common to most if not all of the activities and accumulate without much hedging effect to become very significant at the corporate level. Other risks, like mortality, are pruned somewhat through mutual hedging and diluted when combined into the corporate portfolio.

Economies of Scale

Most insurance activities are characterized by high fixed costs and substantial economies of scale. Insurers with larger volume and market share tend to enjoy larger margins by virtue of lower unit costs and the ability to charge higher premiums and credit lower interest rates.

Many insurance companies strive to expand sales and market share in order not only to spread fixed costs over a larger revenue base but also to derive more influence over their channels of distribution with respect to pricing and allocation of selling effort, thereby increasing margins in the long run. Some marketing executives advocate a consistent policy of competitive pricing to achieve steady growth to a size at which they expect to enjoy this advantage. Broadening the product line is another means of spreading the fixed costs of a distribution channel, especially a career agency force, over a larger revenue base and capturing a larger share of their selling effort and production.

Only the larger companies advertise on national television. By reinforcing their status as "household names," such companies can compete for market share with higher prices (or lower credited interest rates) than less visible competitors. Their access to the retail customer may also be less vulnerable to a downgrade in claims-paying rating than a less well-known company.

The functionality and performance of computer and communications systems have acquired strategic significance as bases for competition, and the price tags of these systems have grown commensurately. Today's best systems not only reduce processing costs but also enhance the ability of an insurer and its distribution system to serve customers, for example, by streamlining the policy issuance process. Some expert underwriting and claims evaluation systems actually outperform skilled personnel while sharply reducing variable costs.

Larger companies also enjoy the advantage of being able to maintain high quality staff professionals in specialized fields of actuarial science, investment management, asset-liability management, systems, and finance. With the growth of accumulation and investment products, investment management skills have become increasingly important. From the perspective of a large company with specialized expertise in all classes of fixed-income securities and first-tier access to securities markets and Wall Street resources, it is difficult to see how an insurer with less that $2 billion of assets can elect to manage its own assets without compromising on investment performance or investment management expenses or both. Above that level, incremental costs of in-house management are low, and access to investment markets improves in terms of the quantity and quality of deal flow and the competitiveness of bid-offer quotations.

A small company typically does not have the same ability as a large company to diversify systematic risk since it does not usually have the choice of being in more than one line of business. Nor can a small insurer build a large enough portfolio of exposures to diversify nonsystematic risks as well as a larger company. At best, a small company can create franchise value by exploiting a marketing or sales niche or a captive customer base, for example, by adopting the strategy of a third-party administrator.

The smaller the company, the greater the dependence on reinsurance and, presumably, the weaker the negotiating position of the ceding company. Because of its size and diversification, the reinsurance market can bear risk much more cheaply than an undiversified insurer. The split of the savings will tend to depend on negotiating power just as it does in the following examples:

- A corporate borrower with access to the A1/P1 commercial paper market can borrow from banks at a rate competitive with that market; a corporate borrower without such ccess pays the prime rate or more.

- A property-casualty insurance customer large enough to access the wholesale markets with a captive insurance operation will enjoy wholesale pricing.

Reinsurance: The Insurer as Risk Intermediary

Reinsurance offers insurers a wholesale market in which risk can be bought or sold, affording the opportunity to grow beyond the capacity of a limited capital base. Considering economies of scale, we can understand why so many companies strive to maximize growth of in-force business and are willing to lay off the risk, and most of the related profit, to the reinsurance markets.

The potential availability of acheiving positive leverage as a risk intermediary makes this strategy all the more appealing. The power of positive leverage is most familiar in the business of real estate investments. Real estate investors and developers use nonrecourse mortgage financing to leverage long-run returns, limit their equity risk, and allow a limited supply of equity to support more projects with greater aggregate return potential. Leverage is positive so long as the after-tax cost of borrowed funds is less than the after-tax return on the asset. Risk is limited to the amount of equity invested so long as the mortgage is nonrecourse.

The benefits of positive leverage and transfer of risk also apply to the use of reinsurance and the use of retrocession by reinsurers. As a risk intermediary, the logical goal of the ceding company is to achieve positive leverage of risk-adjusted returns, where the calculation of return incorporates all relevant costs. It is worth considering whether an insurer's accounting systems and methods of financial analysis provide a realistic estimate of the relevant fixed and variable costs over the projected life of the reinsurance agreement.

In the market for quota-share reinsurance, the price of risk also provides a standard against which to price risk in the primary market. From time to time, we encounter differentials between the direct and reinsurance markets that make one market more attractive than the other. The ability to price rationally and to redirect activity in such circumstances is a key factor for successful management of an intermediary.

Stop-loss reinsurance is designed to limit an insurer's worst-case exposure to loss. Stop-loss reinsurance allows the insurer to assume a greater volume of exposure, with commensurately better diversification of nonsystematic risks. In theory, stop-loss coverage can reduce the risk of insolvency to an arbitrarily low level—a very desirable goal from the perspective of both regulators and stakeholders.

In the financial markets, the equivalent product is options. Bookstaber (1989) has illustrated the insurance-like characteristics of options used by institutions to resculpt risk exposures, and Borch (1990) has observed that equilibrium valuation models for the stop-loss reinsurance and options markets are similar. We will illustrate the use of options as stop-loss reinsurance below.

Just as an insurer hedging with over-the-counter derivative products must consider counter-party default as a source of risk, a ceding company must consider the possible default of the reinsurer as a source of risk. In each case, the risk can be managed by using a diversified portfolio of high-quality counter-parties, negotiating binding documentation that might include exposure-reduction measures that trigger in the event of a material adverse change, and monitoring the "book" of exposure over time for signs of increased vulnerability.

The Insurance Company as Investment Intermediary

One of the activities in our company is selling guaranteed interest contracts (GICs) and group annuities directly to pension plan sponsors and GIC pool managers and investing the proceeds in a diversified, high-quality and liquid fixed-income portfolio. These customized investment products provide features desired by plan sponsors, such as book-value withdrawal under defined circumstances and book-value accounting. Owing to our immunization strategy, underwriting practices and option-pricing and hedging disciplines, the overall exposure to interest-rate risk and adverse interest-rate selection is small.

The activity encompasses the management of the portfolio of assets in relation to the portfolio of liabilities. In effect, this activity is long-term arbitrage between the fixed-income markets and the market for guaranteed pension products. The measure of success must be the net result over time, assessed in relation to risk assumed.

This activity bears the systematic risks of interest-rate changes, unanticipated increases in asset default rates, and mortality. Interest-rate risk includes the component of benefit-responsive withdrawals that might reflect interest-sensitive adverse selection. The risks arising from uncertainty about retirement ages and the noninterest-sensitive component of benefit responsive withdrawals are diversifiable to the extent that they are case-specific as opposed to being driven by the overall state of the economy.

The ideal strategy would provide that in any feasible interest-rate and default-rate scenario, asset returns would exceed the sum of liability returns, expenses and the desired spread. In practice, because the market is competitive, we need to trade off the size of the expected spread against the risk of substandard performance and tolerate some probability of substandard performance within tolerable bounds.

Our ability to sell these products and obtain repeat business depends on meeting customer needs at competitive prices, maintenance of evident financial strength, and excellent processing services, both before and after the sale.

The offering of guaranteed investment products, including GICs, annuities, and universal life, make a life insurance company an investment intermediary and arbitrageur. Like a bank using deposits to make loans or investments and a dealer running a "hedged book" of swaps and other over-the-counter derivative products, a life insurance company assumes a levered exposure to return and risk; as the ratio of assets to capital or surplus is increased, the quality of the future (uncertain) stream of net cash flow and earnings is increasingly sensitive to how the risk and investment "books" are managed. In particular, it becomes increasingly critical to measure realistically and accurately the residual risks retained in the hedged position and to assure that they remain bounded in relation to the surplus or equity employed.

With the rapid growth of investment products over the past decade, a large portion of the investable funds of many life insurance companies is derived from investment product deposits and premiums. In managing risk and return in these spread businesses, insurers should apply the concepts and tools used in other applications of fixed-income arbitrage. Although results at the corporate level are measured by external constituents on the basis of statutory and GAAP earnings, the economic returns and risks are best measured with the tools of fixed-income portfolio analysis. In that framework, liabilities with fixed cash flows can be viewed as short positions in illiquid bonds. Liabilities with interest-sensitive and path-dependent cash flows must, like mortgage-backed securities, be analyzed by simulating alternative interest-rate scenarios.

Recent insurance company failures have illustrated the interplay of interest-rate risk, default risk, and disintermediation or liquidity risk. Many investment products permit customers to redeem or "put" their contracts or policies for cash. This "put" option typically requires payment of a surrender charge; in normal circumstances, customers exercise this option inefficiently, displaying an inertia similar to that exhibited by homeowners reluctant to refinance their mortgages. However, in the event that a problem such as excessive and poorly diversified exposure to risky assets or a large exposure to changes in interest rates causes the insurer's survival to be questioned, the public may become alarmed and the amount of redemptions can far exceed the amount normally expected. Ironically, such a "run on the bank" can force insolvency even in cases in which the assets ultimately prove to be worth more than the liabilities.

Corporate Strategy Decisions

Given the importance of diversification in achieving the best return on capital at the least aggregate risk, an insurance company should evaluate the allocation of its capital resources to risk-bearing activities using the efficient frontier concept commonly employed by pension plan sponsors and consultants to evaluate the allocation of its funds to asset classes. However, insurers should recognize an important difference between the two problems: the latter is a pure portfolio problem concerning classes of assets that, in most cases, are fairly liquid; the former is jointly a portfolio and corporate strategy problem requiring long commitments and illiquid liabilities.

The relative appeal of alternative corporate and activity-level strategies will depend upon the insurer's own market position and areas of competitive strength. Once an insurer decides to focus resources on a given set of activities, development of a competitive advantage can take five to ten years. Most activities and resource commitments cannot be turned on and off or undergo abrupt changes in strategy without undermining market share and efficiency. For example, a decision to increase short-run profits by increasing premiums or reducing credited rates to an abusive extent can undermine the long-term value of goodwill built up with distributors and customers, thereby hurting future sales and profits.

The implication of the characteristically long time frame of insurance products, strategies, resource commitments, and customer relationships is the need to use long-range analysis to fine-tune the critical corporate policy decisions and then focus on implementing these policies successfully and capitalizing on tactical opportunities.

In analyzing the long-run financial consequences of a corporate strategy, it is vital to go beyond current practice in two ways: (1) to use scenario analysis to take uncertainties explicitly into account and (2) to account realistically for the fixed and variable cost structure and capital requirements of the strategy over time, including such costly shared resources as career agency forces and systems.

RECOMENDED ANALYTIC FRAMEWORK

Constraints

The insurance industry must comply with complex state laws and regulations which are intended to protect the customer by assuring maintenance of adequate reserves and surplus. These laws and regulations require periodic filings and detailed record-keeping based on statutory accounting and actuarial valuation standards. This year, in reaction to an increased incidence of insurance company insolvency and liquidity problems, regulators are considering an array of changes to protect customers more effectively.

The better capitalized and more conservative companies welcome the prospect of more discriminating regulation for two reasons. First, failures of marginal companies hurt the industry's image and result in costly assessments of the survivors. Second, the marginal companies tend to engage in aggressive and even irrational pricing practices in order to gain market share, thereby hurting the sales and profits of the more prudent insurers.

Access by insurers to markets of retail and institutional customers is increasingly sensitive to claims-paying ratings, which are also based primarily on statutory filings. Like state laws and regulations, the standards by which the claims-paying abilities of insurers are rated are subject to change, including reaction to whatever problems appear to be at the root of the latest company failure. Accordingly, strategies should be engineered to perform robustly in the event of such contingencies.

Management teams of publicly-held stock insurance companies are also concerned with the cost of equity and debt capital and the retention of control. If two strategies had the same profile of long-run economic results, most management teams would prefer the strategy which tends to generate a stream of earnings that are less volatile and grow more consistently. They would also tend to put extra weight on the financial and operating ratios most closely examined by securities analysts.

Insurers have to respect these constraints. They affect access to markets, the cost of funds and the legal right to remain in business. It follows that in devising or improving a business strategy, an insurer must be concerned not only with achieving economic and financial objectives but also meeting the expectations of these constituents in all time frames in the future. However, a management team that focuses solely on meeting these constraints and pleasing constituents in the short run is unlikely to pursue a strategy with the most favorable long-run consequences for stakeholders.

Existing Practices

Management teams of many insurance companies appear to be trying to maximize growth while complying with externally imposed constraints. As we have seen, size is an advantage with respect to producing at a lower unit cost and enjoying greater control over prices. However, some companies appear to seek growth for growth's sake and to reinforce this objective with performance measurement systems that reward executives for growth even in cases when the incremental profit is inadequate to justify the risk to future profits and possibly survival. There are four related theories that would explain this phenomenon.

The first theory is that insurers, like American corporations in general, focus too much on short-term results at the expense of long-term results and on managing appearances to please constituents at the expense of building wealth for stakeholders. The statutory and GAAP consequences of a more aggressive and risky strategy are likely to be favorable in the early years, particularly if valuation and accounting procedures are aggressive. Such "yield enhancement" investment strategies as writing covered calls enhance current income at the expense of incurring a downwards bias in the market value and earning power of the portfolio.

A second theory is that most insurance executives have acquired their perspective on risk and reward in a regulated industry which has come to rely on regulators, rating agencies and actuaries to evaluate risk and "keep the company out of trouble." Organizations are typically large and bureaucratic. Lacking a realistic, holistic economic model of the firm, top executives tend to focus on the "realities" of achieving sales goals and keeping products competitive, leaving measurement of risk to the actuaries. In the heat of competitive battle, they may expect the investment department to reach for a higher nominal yield in order to achieve sales goals, even though the assets with higher nominal yields may have lower expected returns and more downside risk.

A third theory is based on the concept of agency costs—the cost to the company's stakeholders of the conflict between their interests and those of top management. For the chief executive officer of a mutual company or the CEO of a stock company who had not made a large personal investment in the company, the prospective value of his future compensation and of his stock, if applicable, would be like a call option on the company. This theory seems most appealing in explaining such bizarre practices as concentrating over half the assets of a company with surrenderable deposits into a single risky and illiquid asset class like high-yield bonds or commercial mortgages. Let us suppose this executive is considering a high-growth strategy which will be profitable if things don't go wrong but disastrous if they do. Assuming that the strategy allows the company to conform to external constraints, he has the incentive to "bet the ranch" because his personal downside risk is limited; if an adverse twist of events puts the company under, he can probably move on to another opportunity. Other insurers have written a "put" option requiring them to absorb the excess of claims over asset values.

A fourth theory is that line managers in such companies simply are unaware of the inconsistency of their policies with the long-term interests of their stakeholders. They make decisions using a narrow paradigm that fails to incorporate the consistent evaluation of long-run future consequences of alternative decisions or to take uncertainty into account. The irony is that some companies that appear to be so afflicted have actuarial and investment departments which do some good long-range modeling! It just is not being integrated into the decision processes.

This narrow paradigm perceives safety in familiar practices and risk in the unfamiliar. Unfortunately, the familiar is sometimes risky, like being comfortable with 5% of invested assets in the obligations of one BBB-rated issuer. Similarly, the unfamiliar is sometimes prudent, like the skilled use of listed and over-the-counter derivatives to reduce the risk of operating as an investment intermediary. The goals of policyholders, regulators and stockholders will be well served if the new set of model laws and regulations now being developed are driven by economic reality rather than by this narrow paradigm.

Recommended Statement of Objectives

From a normative perspective, we can think of the stockholders as the primary constituents in a stock company, once obligations to policyholders are met. Stockholders want attractive total returns from a combination of dividends and gains in share values. Over a reasonably long period, these results ought to be consistent with maximizing the risk-adjusted buildup of economic wealth while meeting all constraints, including the avoidance of negative earnings surprises.

In a mutual company, the equity belongs to the policyholders. While recognizing the intergenerational conflicts of interest between past, present and future policyholders, we can say that the entire class of policyholders will derive maximum long-run benefits from strategies that would meet the same objectives as those of a stock company.

A company should try to maximize the risk-adjusted buildup of economic value over an appropriate time frame while satisfying all constraints. The buildup of economic value can be adjusted for risk in a number of different ways. One way is to use a preference function or utility function, varying the coefficient of risk tolerance until the trade-off seems appropriate. Another way is to look at all the outcomes across scenarios and heuristically adjust the strategy to create the most attractive profile of results.

For a given scenario in which future interest rates are specified, economic value can be defined as the net present value of future cash flows to a horizon plus the going-concern value of the firm at that time. Net present value is calculated by discounting the cash flows and terminal value at the specified short-term rates along the scenario. As Becker (1991) has observed, the cash flow available to an owner or holding company from the operations of an insurance company is the distributable statutory income, taking into account the cash required periodically to maintain the desired level of statutory surplus.

Selecting a horizon is a difficult, two-part problem. The first part is choosing the horizon over which to measure the buildup of economic value. The second part is deciding how much further out in time the simulation model must go to estimate terminal value at the end of the first horizon.

The first horizon should be at least five years and preferably ten years because most insurance products have either multi-year life cycles or multi-year profit-and-loss realization periods, or both. Even in the case of short-term products like auto insurance and term-life insurance, a multi-year horizon is necessary to capture the economics of recouping the up-front costs of acquiring a customer by achieving a desirable balance between profit margins and persistence of renewals. Moreover, some of the strategic investment programs of greatest interest and impact take that long to implement and bear fruit, e.g., investment in new technology or strengthening of a national distribution system.

DECISIONS AT THE ACTIVITY LEVEL

Existing Practices

Valuation and pricing actuaries use simulation to measure risk and price products. Although both types of actuaries share similar educational backgrounds and professional training, their roles and perspectives differ.

Valuation actuaries are expected to apply professional standards to the tasks of valuation and risk measurement. Their role is in large part to protect the customer and the public interest from insolvency. At most life insurance companies, valuation actuaries use stochastic techniques to a greater extent than pricing actuaries. With respect to the risk of changing interest rates, cash flow testing under seven specified interest-rate scenarios has been mandated by New York Regulation 126 since 1986 for certain investment products. The Actuarial Standards of Practice now require valuation actuaries to test the adequacy of asset cash flows to cover obligations under a variety of interest-rate scenarios.

As part of operating management, pricing actuaries focus their efforts on the more practical problem of pricing products to meet the combined goals of profitability and volume. They are more likely to use a single scenario of interest rates than a set of scenarios constructed to span the likely range of outcomes. One common calculation is the "asset share," in which the actuary determines the interest-rate spread required to cover fixed and variable expenses, including the amortization of deferred acquisition costs, and earn a targeted profit or return on equity. The motivation behind this static calculation is to conform product pricing to the results promised in operating plans and budgets, which are also generally deterministic.

Decision processes tend to be driven by operating objectives that are defined by a financial plan and budget measured by statutory and possibly GAAP accounting. Management teams are measured by growth in sales and by operating results versus budget. Unfortunately, statutory and GAAP accounting results are based on valuation, reserving and accounting methods that don't fully capture the potential range of long-term consequences of current period decisions. Hence, the influence of current period accounting-driven objectives can be dysfunctional for long-run economic results. This incongruence is most likely to prevail in long-tailed, levered investment product businesses, as we shall see below. Many line executives are not aware of this problem.

Some insurers develop new products and modify existing products primarily with a view to increasing sales. The evaluation of long-run profitability tends to be accomplished after the fact, if at all. For investment spread products, the overriding investment objective is to support the product design with sufficient yield to cover the illustrated credited rate and the margin required for expenses and profit. Many companies drive the investment department to assume a high level of exposure to interest-rate and default risk to achieve the required nominal yield. The adverse consequences of these risks won't be reflected in accounting results until future periods.

Engineering a Strategy with Simulation

For an insurance company, the investment strategy is an integral part of business strategy. The setting of investment objectives, the allocation of assets, and the management of portfolio risk and return are part of a larger decision framework incorporating the design, pricing, sale and management of each type of insurance product and, at the corporate level, the management of the overall portfolio of risk-bearing activities.

The process of developing and testing a new product or of evaluating and improving an existing product results in a *strategy* integrating the product design, the marketing strategy, and a set of decision rules for pricing the product and investing the funds generated. The key factor for success in strategy development is to integrate marketing vision and judgment with realistic, long-range economic analysis taking into account all sources of risk and the frequently complex interplay of fixed and variable costs, as discussed in Chalke (1990).

This crucial process is best accomplished by a task force: A team of product-line, investment and asset-liability management professionals should project the results of existing strategies and consider alternatives that might improve the balance of risk and return. The buildup of skill and insight can become a valuable source of improved decision-making at the operating level.

For existing products, the process might begin with simulation of the consequences of existing strategies, using a "model office" approach to realistically portray the results for a going concern. Concentration on the scenarios for which results are substandard should yield insights into how to improve the strategy. Typically, the design team will encounter a myriad of trade-offs, for example, between achieving a marketable yield and incurring additional interest-rate and or default risk. Simulation provides a laboratory in which these trade-offs can be explored objectively and realistically, provided the right people participate in the project and bring an open perspective.

As an analogue for simulating the results of a complex set of state-contingent and path-dependent decision rules, picture yourself sitting at the controls of a flight simulator. The cockpit provides several instruments that allow you to monitor whether you are maintaining the desired course, altitude, airspeed, attitude, cabin pressure and engine temperature. Keeping these "observables" within tolerance is analogous to meeting constraints. Reaching the destination or target on schedule with the desired margin of fuel is analogous to meeting the economic objective.

Creating a good strategy is analogous to designing an autopilot. To specify a strategy, we need to program decision rules that may depend on all "state variables" and the path we have traveled. The decision rules we program for the autopilot can be modified anytime, at our option, except to the extent that we give up flexibility by entering into written or implied contracts. However, Bellman's Principle of Optimality requires that we specify the state-contingent (and frequently path-dependent) decision rules we believe will be optimal in the future in order to visualize the future consequences of decisions we must make today, as noted in Wagner (1969) and Dixit (1990).

Example: Fixed Single Premium Deferred Annuities

Let us consider a simple example of a strategy simulation for a single premium deferred annuity (SPDA). This SPDA allows the customer to put the policy back to the insurer and get his money back at a declining surrender charge. Like the call or prepayment option retained by a residential mortgage borrower, this "put" option is not exercised "efficiently"; customers tend to exercise the option at a more rapid rate (the "lapse rate") when they have the opportunity to obtain a better deal on another product meeting their needs.

Figure 3 shows a set of assumptions about customer behavior in exercising these "put" options. This family of curves describes the lapse rate on the Y-axis as a function of the gap between what the competitor is offering as a new money rate ("Competitive NMR") versus what we are offering as a renewal rate. The financial incentive to surrender the policy would be measured by the gap, just as the financial incentive to prepay a mortgage is measured by the difference between the coupon on an existing mortgage and the rate on a new mortgage.

FIGURE 3
SPDA Lapse Rate

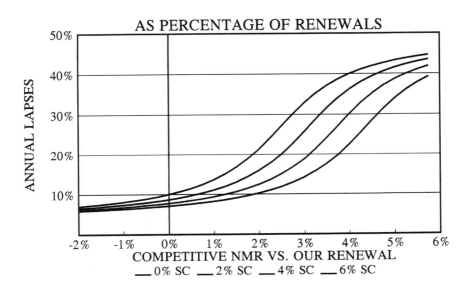

These curves do not reflect "burn-out," which refers to the decline in the lapse rate as the more lapse-prone customers exit the customer population, leaving behind a greater proportion of less lapse-prone customers; we model burn-out as a function of the cumulative opportunity to achieve benefit through a tax-free exchange for a higher-yielding SPDA.

The four different curves represent different levels of surrender charge (0% at the top, 6% at the bottom). Like the call premium on a callable corporate bond, the surrender charge deters withdrawal and partially compensates the issuer for the costs of withdrawal. We model customer behavior as if his incentive to surrender is reduced by the amortized value of the surrender charge, assuming the surrender charge is written off over three years. For example, a person with a 3% surrender charge and a 3% gap would behave the same as a person with a 0% surrender charge and a 2% gap.

Figure 4 shows the results of a simulation in which we tested a particular strategy for setting renewal rates under one very adverse scenario in which the ten-year U.S. Treasury rate rises 5% over a two-year period.

FIGURE 4
Unhedged SPDA Results
With Renewal Rates Subsidized

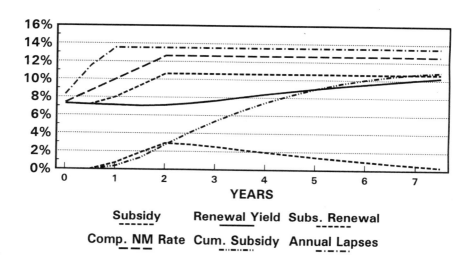

The top curve is the lapse rate—the percentage of policies at the beginning of the year which are going to surrender by the end of the year, an annualized rate.

The next curve is the competitive new money rate, which is assumed to be driven by the ten-year U.S. Treasury yield. The analysis assumes that the carrier invests the net cash flow (the net proceeds of selling new policies, plus the net cash flow from in-force assets and liabilities, less the net outflow to cover lapses) into ten-year maturities.

At the commencement of the simulation, we have been in steady state in a fairly stable interest-rate environment. All bonds have the same yield, the yield is about the same as the prevailing market yield, and we have a laddered portfolio.

Following ten-year Treasuries, the competitive new money rate rises 500 basis points in two years and then levels off. The portfolio yield lags way behind the prevailing market rates because the portfolio matures gradually over a ten-year period. If we had bought seven-year paper, it would catch up more quickly because there would be greater cash flow annually to reinvest at higher yields. In "yield space," the analogue of duration is the speed of adaptation of the portfolio yield to prevailing market rates.

With such a sharp increase in rates, we would face a dilemma; either (1) preserve margins, allow a large gap to result between our renewal rate and the competitive new money rate, and suffer very high lapse rates or (2) pay a higher yield on renewals than the level supported by the portfolio yield, accepting inferior current operating results in order to avoid excessive lapse rates.

Figure 4 illustrates the second alternative. The "subsidized" renewal yield is never allowed to fall more than 200 basis points below the competitive new money rate. With this policy, lapse rates peak at 13.5% per year.

Our subsidy cost is the difference between the subsidized renewal rate and the renewal rate that could be supported by the portfolio yield (the "Renewal Yield" in Figure 4). The annual subsidy peaks at 3% per year and is above 2% for about two and one-half years. Over an eight year period, the cumulative subsidy reaches 11% of assets. That's a painful outcome in a levered, narrow-margin business.

FIGURE 5
SPDAs Hedged With Caps
Cumulative Results

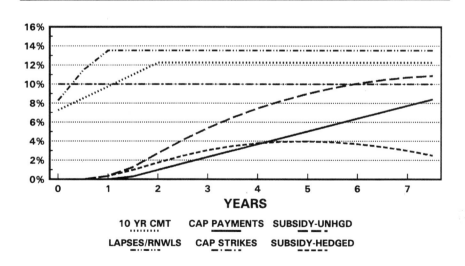

Among the many policy changes we have considered is the use of interest rate caps as "stop loss" reinsurance to hedge against this risk.

Figure 5 shows the results of a cap hedging strategy, using ten-year constant maturity Treasury caps struck at 10%. Under the same assumptions as the previous exhibit, the high-water mark of cumulative subsidy is reduced from 11% to 4%—a more tolerable result.

These exhibits illustrate the use of a simple spreadsheet model to quantify the results of different strategies. To take this kind of research to full fruition, we need a full-scale simulation laboratory allowing us to keep track of a number of different observables and to test decision rules that depend on those observables.

Designing Investment Product Strategies

Figure 6 illustrates the building blocks of an asset-liability strategy. This schematic could serve to illustrate SPDAs, GICs or any other investment product business.

FIGURE 6

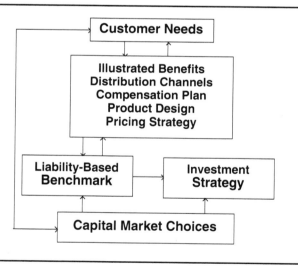

At the top of the chart, we see the customers' needs—e.g., to accumulate money for retirement at a competitive rate and to be able to withdraw the money when necessary or desirable, albeit at a penalty.

In asset-liability management, as in portfolio management, we strive to avoid uncompensated risk and achieve a superior risk-return profile through well-engineered and integrated asset and liability strategies. If we can find a strategy in the bond market that meets the customer's objectives, a product structured around this strategy should be very marketable, while also committing us to pay benefits that are congruent with what we can generate from the investment strategy. That congruence is the key to avoiding uncompensated risk.

For customers who want us to bear risk, e.g., by offering a surrender option without a market-value adjustment clause, we can price that option at or above its cost and offer the product with and without the option. The relevant cost of the option can be estimated analytically or by creating an investment strategy, which might include buying certain options available in the capital markets, such that the income and returns to the strategy cover the benefits payable under the liability in all scenarios.

I use the term "replicating benchmark" interchangeably with "liability-based benchmark" to connote a portfolio that we would own if we were following the investment strategy resulting from the financial engineering process—the strategy found to perform the best in tandem with the liability strategy. This portfolio might consist of generic noncallable, callable and puttable bonds of various maturity dates and the most fundamental option and swap structures available in the capital markets.

As illustrated in Figure 7, the replicating benchmark is the end product of the financial engineering process. It links that process with the investment management process. Commercially available asset-liability models are typically more functional for liabilities than for assets. Using generic assets simplifies the modeling process with minimal loss of accuracy; the simplification makes simulation of multiple scenarios less time-consuming and allows use of parameters like maturity and duration to expedite testing of alternative strategies and to make application of optimization tractable.

FIGURE 7

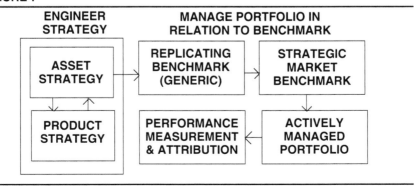

ENGINEER STRATEGY	MANAGE PORTFOLIO IN RELATION TO BENCHMARK	
ASSET STRATEGY	REPLICATING BENCHMARK (GENERIC)	STRATEGIC MARKET BENCHMARK
PRODUCT STRATEGY	PERFORMANCE MEASUREMENT & ATTRIBUTION	ACTIVELY MANAGED PORTFOLIO

The core challenge of strategy engineering is to discover what generic investment strategy, together with a strategy for operating the product, would result in a scenario profile that creates an attractive level of return in relation to the downside risk across all scenarios. Generally, the markets are too competitive and the products too complex to allow a perfectly uniform pattern of positive net cash flows across all scenarios. The more practical statement of the problem is to require that the results be no worse than a certain level to the horizon and in any period. Stop-loss reinsurance and options can be considered as tools for meeting this set of constraints.

Simulation

Simulation should be our core analytical tool because of the path-dependent behavior of assets and liabilities with interest-sensitive cash flows. Path dependence creates the need for dynamic or adaptive strategies, i.e., for path and state-dependent decision rules. Simulation allows consideration of such strategies, including the use of option replication and other dynamic hedging methods as alternatives to up-front purchase of options.

Simulation also has the desirable property of allowing us to keep track of multiple observables required to monitor compliance with constraints as well as to compute the risk-adjusted value (i.e., utility) of scenario results, i.e., periodic cash flows, statutory and GAAP earnings, and net capital requirements. Hence, simulation allows us to evaluate and rank results by scenario and across scenarios using a variety of measures.

In the simulation model, the outer loop is the scenario, and the inner loop is each discrete point in time. Within these loops, we need the functionality to simulate all the moving parts:

- the evolution of interest rates and other risk sources over time,

- the competitors' new money and renewal rates,

- the decision rules governing the new money and renewal rates to be credited and the investment of new deposits and cash flows from in-force business,

- the resulting behavior of customers—new sales, deposits on existing contracts, and surrenders, and

- accounting for all of the results or "observables."

Figure 8 illustrates different uses of simulation and the kinds of scenario samples suitable for each use. Working with single scenarios can produce great insights. Once a tentative strategy is developed, however, we need a sample whose paths span the space of feasible realizations in the term structure realistically while being sufficiently parsimonious to allow the computer to process complex decision rules and calculations at each time step.

FIGURE 8
Uses of Simulation
And Types of Path Samples

	Ad Hoc	Structured (LPS)	Monte Carlo
What if?	X	X	
Prob. wtd. results	X	X	X
Calculate OAS		X	X
Optimize strategy	X	X	
Price options		X	X

If we want to price bonds accurately and get a realistic probability-weighted profile of results, we can use either a sufficiently large random sample (Monte Carlo) or a smaller, more economical structured sample like the linear path space (LPS) proposed in Ho (1992). LPS captures the risk related to the term structure of interest rates efficiently and produces reasonably accurate results for many problems with as few as 50 to 150 paths; accuracy is much greater than would be obtained with a random sample consisting of the same number of paths.

Monte Carlo scenarios generated with proper methodology, as discussed in Tilley (1991), will preserve bond prices and option prices and be arbitrage free. Monte Carlo simulation with large samples can be used to test and calibrate more parsimonious methods like LPS.

When we use interest-rate scenarios to test the consequences and measure the risk of alternative asset-liability strategies, should the paths necessarily be arbitrage free? In other words, should the term structure of forward rates and volatilities implied by today's bond and option prices govern the scenarios used to engineer strategies? If we are going to use arbitrage-free paths for interest rates, then should we also use arbitrage-free paths for mortality and morbidity? As risk intermediaries, should we be pricing mortality relative to the reinsurance cost?

The answers to these questions depend on the purpose of the analysis. For relative pricing, we must use arbitrage-free scenarios. However, for testing the long-run risks of a strategy, the crucial need is to capture realistically the range of outcomes that might occur. The rationality of using expected utility as a tool for decision-making is based on subjective probabilities, as proposed in Raiffa (1965). Hence, the issue brings us back to deciding whether the rates and volatilities implied by the market represent the best information about the probability distribution of future interest rates.

Considering the empirical research findings that forward rates have limited predictive power, it is tempting to apply a Bayesian approach to the estimation of long-term mean rates and volatilities. If the implied forward rates and volatilities don't look reasonable, we can impose our own views in the form of a "prior" distribution and treat the implied data as a sample.

Evaluating Scenario Profiles

To allow ranking of one strategy versus another, we must identify the measures of results and criteria for success, and translate the objectives into an explicit preference function that we can apply to the profile of results across scenarios. This function may be used as the objective function in the application of optimization within a scenario framework.

The net present value of cash flows to the horizon, including terminal value, is a key output variable for which we want to examine the profile and related probabilities. But we also need to look at the quality of the ride, in terms of the low water mark of economic wealth (called "drawdown" by traders) and such constraints as earnings quality, statutory capital requirements, and maintenance of debt and claims paying ratings.

The need to evaluate multiple dimensions of performance, account for risk, and check for compliance with constraints over multiple time periods leads to the idea of using a preference function that would assign a numeric score to a combination of observed results. The preference function captures our overall feelings about the consequences of the strategy in a given scenario. The profile of scores across a set of scenarios allow us to determine whether the overall results of one strategy are preferable to those of another strategy.

Several authors have proposed the use of mathematical programming to seek the optimum strategy within the framework of pathwise results (see Ho (1992) and Hiller and Schaack (1990)). Such optimization models require the specification of a single objective function, such as minimizing the cost of an initial portfolio which has the desired probability of covering the liability cash flows. A utility function allow us to trade off risk and reward in the objective function.

THE CORPORATE LEVEL

Rolling Up Scenario Results

The simulations of strategies at the activity level must be "rolled up" scenario-by-scenario to the corporate level to capture the effects of diversification and to reveal opportunities to improve the overall balance of risk and return. To allow results to be rolled up by scenario, an insurer must use the same scenarios for each activity, as shown in Figure 9. If the detailed results for each activity are stored by scenario, they may subsequently be combined in various ways to reveal exposures of parts of the company and the whole company.

FIGURE 9

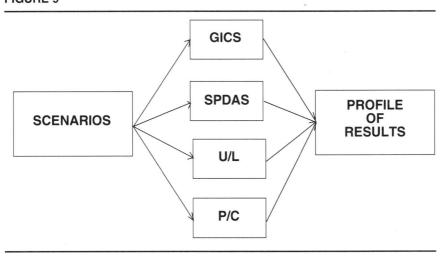

If an insurance company is owned by a holding company, the rollup should be done at both the legal entity level and the holding company level. At the legal entity level, the relevant issues are periodic statutory compliance, net capital requirements, and maintenance of desired claims-paying ratings. At the holding company level, the relevant issues are the long-term risk-adjusted build-up of economic wealth on an after-tax basis, reflecting the filing of a consolidated tax return, if applicable.

Some companies maintain costly shared resources like a career agency force. If this resource is shared by several activities, but not all activities, then it is important to roll up the scenario results of activities that use the resource and reflect the cost of that resource in the results. The goal should be to identify a set of strategies for these activities that achieves the best combined profile of results. It is likely that the optimum strategy will make good use of that resource and leverage its productivity over time.

It is also useful to aggregate activities with similar risk patterns, e.g., investment products with fixed cash flows, investment products with interest-sensitive cash flows, and noninvestment products. To the extent that the company has an undue concentration of exposure to a particular source of risk, the study of the activities contributing this risk can focus attention on trading off the relative return versus risk of each activity and on selecting which activity or activities should be considered candidates for reduction or divestiture. Reinsurance could also be considered in this framework.

Analysis of rolled-up results at these various levels will reveal not only imbalances in the corporate portfolio but also the need to reevaluate the activity-level strategies and to consider alternative corporate-level decisions regarding reinsurance and the use of derivative products. For example, the discovery that the company is overly exposed to rising interest rates might lead to consideration of investing in shorter maturities, buying interest-rate caps, reducing the growth in annuity sales, reinsuring annuity sales, or redesigning annuity products.

The rolled-up results will highlight risk factors to which exposure is excessive and risk factors with respect to which the company has "slack," in a mathematical programming sense. If the corporate strategy problem were structured as a portfolio optimization problem, the shadow prices and other results could provide valuable insights that could guide the construction of a good hedge and provide valuable feedback to the activity level about the corporation's marginal tolerances for each source of risk.

Identifying Risk Factors

In seeking a more efficient corporate portfolio, an insurer must treat most of the systematic risk factors as multidimensional factors to which exposure can be positive or negative, allowing for mutual hedging of activities. In theory, we can extend the concept of dollar-duration as a measure of the price risk induced by an instantaneous parallel shift in the yield curve and measure the instantaneous sensitivity of capital (or the net present value of future profits) to changes in each of these factors. To normalize the amount of risk contributed by these disparate factors, we might quantify the effect of a one standard deviation and two standard deviation adverse experience in each factor.

Interest rate exposure could be summarized in terms of vectors of key rate durations and convexities, as proposed in Ho (1990) and Reitano (1991). Our GIC asset portfolio might have the same effective dollar-duration as the liability portfolio, but if the timing of cash flows were different, as in the case of a bullet-barbell mismatch, the net cash flow from the hedged portfolio would be sensitive to nonparallel movements in the yield curve. Such movements are captured by key rate durations, which measure the sensitivity of a bond's price to changes in each of 11 segments of the yield curve. Similarly, to the extent that the options embedded in the assets did not hedge those embedded in the liabilities exactly, the net cash flow stream would be vulnerable to volatility in the yield curve.

Asset default exposure could be represented by a factor model in which the exposure to an unanticipated increase in the riskiness of industry i or sector j could be expressed by the sum, over all holdings in that industry or sector, of the product of the amount invested in that sector or industry times its riskiness (reflecting rating, position in the capital structure, etc.), where riskiness is analogous to the factor beta in the arbitrage pricing model. Estimation of aggregate risk would require combining all sectors or industries so as to capture the entire covariance matrix, recognizing the significant correlations between sectors and industries engendered by common macroeconomic forces.

Mortality exposure could be represented by a term structure model which captures exposure to increases or decreases in estimated current and future mortality rates broken down into cells defined by age, gender, and other relevant demographic characteristics. The risk of a block of life insurance in a given year would be found by summing the products for each cell of dollar exposure (reflecting excess-loss coverage) times risk.

Most activities are exposed to several sources of risk. Even a company that sells only term life insurance can diversify its portfolio of risk exposures by (1) assuming some risks to earn increased returns from the investment portfolio, (2) using excess-loss and quota-share reinsurance to avoid an undue concentration of exposure to mortality, and (3) assuring that its book of mortality risk is well diversified demographically.

Some of those risk sources are more correlated at the tails of the distributions than under typical circumstances. For example, a large earthquake or tornado can systematically skew loss ratios for many property and casualty lines that, when examined statistically, appear relatively uncorrelated. When managing a levered intermediary, it is critical to consider exposures at the tails of the distributions and on the possible unexpected events that cause experience to approach these tails. Deterministic simulation—with one scenario at a time—is an excellent tool for stress-testing the company's ability to survive such events and for assessing the need for stop-loss reinsurance.

IMPLEMENTATION: STRATEGY FOR MANAGING CHANGE

If the results of such analysis are to be translated into action, corporate and line-of-business executives must buy into, sponsor and participate in the analytic process and make it an integral part of the decision process. Obtaining this executive sponsorship and involvement is a major challenge requiring a patient process of education at all levels of management. In practice, the achievement of good results in a series of projects attracts the interest of executives and serves to build demand for more widespread use of economic simulation. Direct involvement by marketing and product executives is key to implementation of project results.

Unfortunately, there are some obstacles to implementation deeply embedded in organization structure, management processes, and corporate culture. Even with the commitment of the chief executive officer, the integration of economic modeling into the decision process requires skillful management of organizational and cultural change, including the recasting of corporate and line-of-business objectives, performance measurement standards and compensation plans. It also requires a fundamental shift in the strategic paradigm, recognizing the need for a longer horizon and a focus on the risk-adjusted build-up of economic wealth.

Top management participation in the corporate review is critical. The insights gained from the corporate rollup of scenario results can lead to consideration of a variety of policy changes that could profoundly affect the long-run results of the company.

The increased role of stochastic economic modeling in decision-making should increase the realism and economic sensitivity of the decision processes at all levels. It then remains to close the loop by tying performance measurement standards to the resulting objectives and policies. One of the greatest challenges in a decentralized organization is assuring that the line-of-business manager has the incentive to act in the best interests of the company as a whole, in terms of the balance of short versus long run goals, economic versus "cosmetic" goals, and departmental versus corporate level of risk-aversion. This can only be accomplished if objectives are set and performance is measured in a manner consistent with long-range stochastic economic modeling. While this is arguably true in most businesses, it is especially true in the insurance business.

REFERENCES

Asay, Michael R., Peter J. Bouyoucos, and Anthony M. Marciano, 1989, An economic approach to valuation of single premium deferred annuities, Goldman, Sachs & Co.

Babbel, David F., Thomas A. McAvity, Jr., Reed P. Miller, and James F. Reiskytl, 1990, Product features versus investment policy, *Record of the Society of Actuaries,* San Francisco Meeting.

Babbel, David F., Robert Stricker, and Irwin T. Vanderhoof, 1990, Performance measurement for insurers, Goldman, Sachs & Co.

Babbel, David F., and Robert Stricker, 1987, Asset/liability management for insurers, Goldman Sachs & Co.

Becker, David N., 1991, A method for option-adjusted pricing and valuation of insurance products, *Product Development News* (November), Society of Actuaries.

Becker, David N.,1988, A generalized profits released model for the measurement of return on investment for life insurance, *Transactions of the Society for Actuaries* Vol. XL.

Borch, Karl H., 1990, *Economics of Insurance* (Elsevier, Amsterdam).

Chalke, Shane A., 1990, Macro pricing: Toward a comprehensive product development process, Chalke, Incorporated.

Dixit, Avinash K., 1990,*Optimization in Economic Theory* (Oxford University Press, New York).

Hiller, Randall S. and Christian Schaack, 1990, A classification of structured bond portfolio modeling techniques, *The Journal of Portfolio Management* Fall.

Ho, Thomas S. Y., 1990, *Strategic Fixed-Income Investment* (Dow Jones-Irwin, Homewood, IL).

Ho, Thomas S. Y., and Sang-Bin Lee, 1986, Term structure movements and pricing interest rate contingent claims, *Journal of Finance* Vol. 41, No. 5 1986.

Ho, Thomas S. Y., 1992, Managing illiquid bonds and the linear path space, *Journal of Fixed Income* June.

Huang, Chi-fu and Robert H. Litzenberger, 1988, *Foundations for Financial Economics*, (North-Holland).

Leibowitz, Martin L., Stanley Kogelman, and Lawrence N. Bader, 1990, Asset performance and surplus control: A dual-shortfall approach, Salomon Brothers Publication.

Noris, Peter D., 1989, Multifactor immunization, Morgan Stanley.

Pedersen, Hal W., Elias S. W. Shiu, and A. E. Thorlacius, 1989, Arbitrage-free pricing of interest-rate contingent claims, *Transactions of the Society of Actuaries*.

Raiffa, Howard, 1968, *Decision Analysis* (Addison Wesley, Reading, MA).

Reitano, Robert R., 1991, Multivariate duration analysis, *Transactions of the Society of Actuaries*.

Tilley, James A., 1991, An actuarial layman's guide to building stochastic interest rate generators, *Transactions of the Society of Actuaries*, Volume 44.

Wagner, Harvey M., 1969, *Principles of Operations Research* (Prentice-Hall, Inc., Englewood Cliffs, NJ).

Zurcher, Michael L., FSA, 1991, Target surplus formulas take center stage as financial drama unfolds, *Reinsurance Reporter* Second Quarter.